INAUGURAL CAVALCADE

☆ ☆ ☆

INAUGURAL CAVALCADE

☆ ☆ ☆

Louise Durbin

Illustrated with photographs and old prints

*The honor of your presence
is requested at the ceremonies attending the
Inauguration of the President
of the United States*

DODD, MEAD & COMPANY · NEW YORK

Illustrations courtesy of:
Architect of the Capitol, 70; Author's Collection, 5, 90; Dwight D. Eisenhower Library, Abilene, Kansas, 177 *top*; Franklin D. Roosevelt Library, Hyde Park, New York, 163, 164 *top*; Harry S. Truman Library, Independence, Missouri, 170; The James Monroe Museum and Memorial Library, Fredericksburg, Virginia, 28; John F. Kennedy Library, Waltham, Massachusetts, 181 *top*; The Ladies' Hermitage Association, Hermitage, Tennessee, 37; Library of Congress, xiv, 6 *bottom*, 12, 16, 17, 18, 23, 24, 25, 35 *bottom*, 38, 43 *bottom*, 44, 48 *bottom*, 49, 50, 53, 56, 58, 63, 65, 69, 72, 73, 74, 77, 79, 81, 82, 87, 92 *top*, 94, 96, 98 *top*, 106, 108 *bottom*, 113, 115, 121, 122, 124, 129, 130, 131, 133, 136, 137, 138, 141, 146, 154, 157; Library of Congress, Frances Benjamin Johnston Collection, 126, 127; Library of Congress, French Collection, 152; The Mount Vernon Collection, Courtesy The Mount Vernon Ladies' Association, 10; National Archives, 13, 54, 64, 85, 88, 132, 142, 143, 144, 148, 156, 158, 160, 162, 165, 171; National Archives, Brady Collection, 29; National Gallery of Art, Gift of Edgar William & Bernice Chrysler Garbisch, 6 *top*; National Park Service, U.S. Department of the Interior, 26, 92 *bottom*, 164 *bottom*, 166, 169, 173, 177 *bottom*, 178, 179, 186, 190, 192; National Portrait Gallery 35 *top*, 43 *top*, 47; New York Public Library, 32 *right*; New York Public Library, Phelps Stokes Collection, 33, 40; *Perley's Reminiscences*, 45, 61, 97, 99; Polk Home, Columbia, Tennessee, Courtesy James Knox Polk Memorial Auxiliary, 59; The Rutherford B. Hayes Library, Fremont, Ohio, 102, 103, 105, 109, 110; The Smithsonian Institution, iii, 9, 20, 32 *left*, 36, 39, 60, 67, 78, 83, 84, 98 *bottom*, 100, 112, 119, 134, 139; The Smithsonian Institution, from the Ralph E. Becker Collection of Political Americana, 3, 48 *top*, 76, 104, 108 *top*, 118, 161; The Smithsonian Institution, photograph by Al Robinson, 198; U.S. Air Force Photo, 189 *bottom*; U.S. Army Photograph, 147, 172, 175, 176, 181 *bottom*, 182, 183, 184, 191, 194, 196, 197; U.S. Army Photograph, by Cecil Stoughton, 185, 189 *top*; Vermont Development Department, 150, 151; The White House Collection, Courtesy White House Historical Association, 14, 22.

ISBN: 0-396-06421-3

Library of Congress Catalog Card Number: 76-162611

Printed in the United States of America

To My Father
SAMUEL CLYDE DURBIN

"The true test of civilization is, not the census, nor the size of the cities, nor the crops—no, but the kind of man the country turns out."

—Ralph Waldo Emerson, from *"Civilization"*

ACKNOWLEDGMENTS

☆ ☆ ☆

For their interest, encouragement, and assistance the author is indebted to many people in the preparation of this book. First, the author wishes to extend her deepest appreciation to Margaret Brown Klapthor, to Betty Dickman, and to Norah Smaridge for reading the manuscript or the outline of this book and for offering valuable suggestions. As for the many others who have contributed in some way to *Inaugural Cavalcade*, beginning with the anonymous chroniclers of the early inaugurations, the author takes this opportunity to thank them, one and all, and express her gratitude especially to the following individuals and institutions.

Alice Roosevelt Longworth (Mrs. Nicholas Longworth)
Elinor Lee (Mrs. Weymer Lee)
Elisabeth Stevens (Mrs. Robert Schleussner)
The James Monroe Memorial Foundation: Laurence Gouverneur Hoes, President
Rutherford B. Hayes Library: Watt P. Marchman, Director
Franklin D. Roosevelt Library: James O'Neill, Director
John F. Kennedy Library: Carolyn O'Leary, Librarian
Dwight D. Eisenhower Library: W. A. Scott, Staff Photographer
Harry S. Truman Library: Philip D. Lagerquist, Research Archivist
James Knox Polk Memorial Auxiliary: Mrs. O. B. Quin, President
The Ladies' Hermitage Association: Douglas Green, Research Assistant
Andrew Johnson National Historic Site: Hugh A. Lawing, Historian
The Calvin Coolidge Memorial Foundation, Inc.: Sally Thompson, Executive Secretary
United States Department of Defense: Bettie Sprigg
Smithsonian Institution: Margaret Brown Klapthor and Herbert R. Collins, Associate Curators, Division of Political History

ACKNOWLEDGMENTS

District of Columbia Public Library: Sue Shivers, Washingtoniana Room

Office of the Architect of the Capitol: George M. White, Architect of the Capitol, and Florian Thayn, Head of Research and Reference Service

Library of Congress: Renata Shaw and Virginia Daiker, Prints and Photographs Division

Pierce Homestead; The Mount Vernon Ladies' Association; White House Historical Association; National Archives; National Gallery of Art; National Park Service; National Portrait Gallery; Vermont Development Department; New York Public Library; Buffalo and Erie County Historical Society; Library of Congress: Manuscript Division, Rare Books Division, and Newspaper Reading Room; *The Washington Post*

Massachusetts Historical Society: Quotations from the unpublished Adams Papers are from the microfilm edition, by permission of the Massachusetts Historical Society.

PREFACE

☆ ☆ ☆

"Before he enter on the Execution of his Office," reads the last sentence in Article II, Section 1, of the Constitution, "he shall take the following Oath or Affirmation:—'I do solemnly swear (or affirm) that I will faithfully execute the Office of President of the United States, and will to the best of my Ability, preserve, protect and defend the Constitution of the United States.'"

It was a simple formula for the inauguration of a President when it was written in 1787, and so it remains today. Time-honored traditions now surround the oath-taking, but the unpretentious ceremony is, in essence, at the very heart of the democratic process, the grand experiment initiated by the Founding Fathers. A private citizen repeats the 35-word oath and in that dramatic moment becomes the President of the United States, endowed with the awesome duties and powers of that office, elevated by his fellow citizens—both those who have elected him and those who have willingly acquiesced to the verdict of the election by the people.

There have been inaugurations during the aftermath of jubilant victory and under the shadow of war, by the light of a kerosene lamp in a Vermont village, before thousands clustered around the east portico of the Capitol, and before a handful of witnesses following the assassinations of four Presidents. In each case, with the 35-word oath the power of the nation passed into the hands of the rightful successor to the Presidency. Throughout there has been a peaceful continuity in change, despite the trauma of the times, and though this transition of power may be taken for granted today, in the early days of the republic it was recognized as being an extraordinary event in the history of nations.

"In some countries such a transfer of power would have cost streams of blood, and shaken the Government to its very foundations," noted *The National Intelligencer* writer who witnessed the ceremony at the

Capitol when Millard Fillmore succeeded to the Presidency following the death of President Zachary Taylor in July, 1850.

The aim of this book is to bring into vivid focus the inaugurations of the thirty-six men who have held the highest, loneliest job in the land as the President of the United States. Time and space have limited the details which have been carefully selected to give both a capsule history of the inaugural ceremonies and festivities for each President and occasional fleeting glimpses of contemporary events, for an inauguration does not take place in a vacuum.

We want to see these men and their inaugurations through the eyes of their fellow citizens, and to the people of the period who left behind them diaries, letters, memoirs, and newspapers and periodicals I am deeply in debt for the fascinating details and anecdotes in *Inaugural Cavalcade*. It is through these intimate glimpses behind the formal inaugural ceremonies that I have sought to convey the humanity, the humor, the grief and the glory that have been part of inaugural dramas since George Washington's first inauguration over 180 years ago.

L.D.

CONTENTS

☆ ☆ ☆

CONTENTS

INAUGURAL CAVALCADE

☆　☆　☆

The inauguration of George Washington as President of the United States, April 30, 1789, at Federal Hall, New York City. This engraving, made by Amos Doolittle after a drawing by Peter Lacour, is the only known contemporary rendition of the first inauguration.

GEORGE WASHINGTON

☆ ☆ ☆

April 30, 1789   March 4, 1793

On April 30, 1789, Chancellor Robert Livingston of New York stepped to the gilded iron bannister of Federal Hall's balcony, which overlooked Broad and Wall Streets in New York City, and shouted, "Long live George Washington, President of the United States!"

A thunderous ovation answered from the multitude of citizens who dangled precariously out of windows, perched on roofs, and crowded the streets below so densely that it seemed possible to walk on the heads of the people.

The balcony was in full view of the assembled throng. It was a strange mixture of the elegant and the scrubby, toothless old people and rose-cheeked young ones, and middle-aged Revolutionary War veterans. All shared in the triumphal rejoicing, for it was on this bright, spring day that George Washington took the oath of office as the first President of the United States.

Citizens of New York had contributed $32,000 to transform the old City Hall into the Federal Hall and the open balcony made a dramatic stage. In the ornamental design, architect Pierre L'Enfant had included, in the triangular pediment over the balcony, a great American eagle, with the shield of the United States emblazoned on its body and with thirteen arrows and an olive branch clutched in its talons.

In the center of the balcony was a red velvet-covered table topped by a crimson velvet cushion on which lay a large, red, morocco-bound Bible with gilt ornamentation and silver clasps. Unknown to the spectators, the elegant Bible had been borrowed at the last minute from St. John's Masonic Lodge in the City Assembly Rooms nearby, when Chancellor

Livingston discovered there wasn't a Bible to be found in Federal Hall. Only this brilliant bit of paraphernalia was on hand when, about one in the afternoon, George Washington, the President-elect, stepped from the Senate Chamber onto the balcony, accompanied by John Adams, the Vice President, New York Governor George Clinton, Chancellor Livingston, and the other distinguished witnesses.

As the joyous cheers met him, General Washington walked to the front of the balcony, laid his hand on his heart, and bowed several times. He was a striking figure, over six feet two, "with the native dignity and with that urbanity so peculiarly combined in the character of a soldier and eminent private gentleman," wrote a contemporary. On this day he wore a dark brown suit, manufactured in Hartford, Connecticut, with metal buttons stamped with an eagle in relief, white silk stockings, low shoes and silver shoe buckles, with a steel-hilted dress sword at his side. "His hair was dressed and powdered in the fashion of the day and worn in a bag and solitaire," Washington Irving recalled years later, remembering how, as a boy of six, he had looked down from the corner of New and Wall Streets upon the first inauguration.

The throng seemed to sense that Washington was overwhelmed by the scene before him and became still. Washington turned and sat down in a chair near the table for a few moments. Then he rose and came forward. The Secretary of the Senate, Samuel Alyne Otis, held the open Bible on the crimson cushion as Chancellor Livingston read the oath prescribed by the Constitution. With his right hand on the Bible, Washington repeated the 35-word oath while the people, hushed in reverent silence, listened: "I do solemnly swear that I will faithfully execute the office of President of the United States and will to the best of my ability preserve, protect and defend the Constitution of the United States."

Then, with a depth of feeling marked by all, he added, "I swear, So Help Me God." The chancellor lifted the Bible and the first President bent forward to kiss the book.

"It is done," said Chancellor Livingston as he turned to the throng in the streets, waved his hand, and cried: "Long live George Washington, President of the United States!"

The raising of the flag signaled a discharge of artillery from the battery. "All the bells in the city rang out a peal of joy, and the multitude before us sent forth such a shout as seemed to rend the skies," recalled a 17-year-old girl who had watched the unforgettable scene.

The President bowed repeatedly to the people and then went into the

Copper buttons, souvenirs of Washington's first inauguration which actually took place on April 30, 1789, instead of "March the Fourth 1789" as the eagle-centered button on the left indicates. At right, within the linked ovals forming a circular chain, are the initials of the original thirteen states, with "GW" for George Washington centering the inner circle that proclaims "Long Live the President."

Senate Chamber to make his inaugural address before the combined Houses of Congress. The chamber, too, had been handsomely decorated with designs in keeping with the building's Federal character, a sun and thirteen stars having been painted on the light blue ceiling. Rich crimson damask fashioned the canopy over the President's elevated platform, the curtains, and the chair seats.

Overwhelmed by the emotion of the moment, "this great man was agitated and embarrassed more than ever he was by the leveled cannon or pointed musket," one observer remarked. Washington trembled, and his deep voice was low and his manner grave, almost sad.

After delivering his inaugural address, the President, accompanied by the Vice President, the two Houses of Congress and all their officers, walked over to St. Paul's Church for special services. The military lined the street as the Bishop of the Episcopal Church of New York and Chaplain of the Senate, Samuel Provost, conducted prayers for the new nation. Following the service, the President entered the state coach which had carried him to Federal Hall and was escorted home, for a short respite only. The celebrations of the great event were far from over. The great occasion had been a long time coming and everyone wanted to savor every moment of the memorable day.

3

It was thirteen years since men from the thirteen colonies had signed the Declaration of Independence. During the war, the Articles of Confederation had joined the thirteen fledgling states into "a firm league of friendship" against the common foe and former mother country, Great Britain. The new Constitution called for a stronger, federal government, with executive power vested in a President to be elected by special electors, to be appointed by each of the states.

At sunset on March 3, 1789, thirteen guns had been fired from Fort George to signal the demise of the old Confederation. On the following morning, the new Federal era was ushered in by the firing of eleven guns, for only eleven states had up to that time adopted the Constitution. Bell-ringing and eleven-gun salutes punctuated the day, but only eight Senators and thirteen Representatives were on hand for the joint session of Congress at noon—not enough for the quorum necessary to do business.

By April 6 both Houses of Congress had a quorum and the members met for the sole purpose of counting the votes cast by the sixty-nine electors. George Washington of Virginia was unanimously elected President. John Adams of Massachusetts was declared Vice President with the next highest number—thirty-four—of votes cast, a triumph over ten competitors. Only ten states cast electoral votes for the first President, for New York's Governor Clinton had neglected, because of his Anti-Federalist sympathies, to appoint electors for his state.

Charles Thomson, an Irish-born Philadelphia schoolteacher and secretary of the old Continental Congress, set off the next day for Washington's plantation, Mount Vernon on the Potomac, to carry the notice of election to the General. Sylvanus Bourne had the honor of undertaking the mission to Adams in Braintree, Massachusetts.

Thomson arrived at Mount Vernon on April 14. Two days later at ten o'clock in the morning, General Washington bid his wife, Martha, goodbye and set out in his elegant cream-colored coach accompanied by Thomson and Colonel David Humphreys, his aide-de-camp. The coach had barely rolled out of the coachyard before it was met by Washington's neighbors and friends who escorted him to nearby Alexandria for the first of the magnificent dinners and tributes that marked his week's triumphal cavalcade to New York. Washington's political opponents, the Anti-Federalists, declared that equality and the liberties of the people were doomed and accused Washington of courtly ambitions.

John Adams, too, was given a splendid send-off from his native Massachusetts, and in Connecticut both Hartford and New Haven gentlemen

On the bridge at Trenton, over which General Washington had retreated during the Revolutionary War, the women of Trenton, with their young daughters dressed in white, awaited the hero on his way to be inaugurated. While the ladies sang an original ode, the maidens scattered flowers before Washington, who later sent a handwritten note of appreciation to the group.

on horseback rode out to escort him into their cities. But when Adams arrived in New York City on April 21, no living arrangements had been made for the Vice President. "Our countrymen's idea of the 'L'air imposant' is yet confined to volunteer escorts, verbal compliments, etc.," he grumbled in a letter to his wife. He went off, trailing quite a respectable escort of cavalry and distinguished citizens, to be the houseguest of his good friend, Secretary of State John Jay. The day following his arrival, Adams was escorted to the Senate Chamber in Federal Hall, and there he gave a brief address, quietly took the oath of office, and assumed his duties as Vice President of the United States.

On the very day that Washington arrived in New York, April 23, a serious debate was taking place in both Houses of Congress over the title and form of address for the Chief Magistrate of the infant government. Adams favored: "His Highness, the President of the United States and

Salute to General Washington in New York Harbor, painted by L. M. Cooke about 1875, now is in the National Gallery of Art, Washington, D.C. It was a gift of Edgar William and Bernice Chrysler Garbisch.

The first presidential mansion was the Franklin house at No. 1 Cherry Street, New York City.

Protector of their Liberties." Some preferred "His Serene Highness" or "His Excellency," others plain "Mr. Washington." Eventually the first joint Congressional committee, appointed to confer on titles and the ceremony for the inauguration, decided that the Chief Magistrate's title should be simply, "The President of the United States." And so it remains.

Washington arrived in New York aboard a magnificent barge, made especially to transport him up the bay from Elizabethtown Point, New Jersey, to New York. Thirteen masters of vessels, dressed in white uniforms and black caps ornamented with fringes, were at the oars of the barge which embarked at high noon to the cracking of artillery, and boat after boat, gaily decked out in all their naval ornaments, fell into the hero's train, making a splendid appearance.

The stairs at Murray's Wharf, near the Coffee House, were covered with carpeting and the rails draped in crimson when the elegant barge drew up about three o'clock. Washington, wearing a blue coat, buff waistcoat and breeches, stepped ashore as cannons boomed and the bells of the city rang. Then he by-passed both the honor guard and the carriage waiting for him and walked through the crowded streets, attended by Governor Clinton and others, to the Franklin House at No. 1 Cherry Street which had been redecorated for the President's residence. He received men who swarmed to pay their affectionate respects and then, without changing clothes, he went to dine at the Governor's house. Even rain in the evening did not dampen the spirits of the ranks who milled through the superbly illuminated streets. It had been a "day of extravagant joy," an observer noted, and it seemed impossible that inauguration day itself could surpass this one for sheer splendor. A week later, it did.

By the twenty-ninth of April, visitors crowded every private house, as well as taverns and boardinghouses, and many slept in tents. The roar of artillery at sunrise from old Fort George announced the great day at last, April 30, which was gray and overcast in the morning.

At nine o'clock, all the church bells in the city rang for half an hour and the people gathered in their places of worship to say prayers for the safety of the President and to seek the blessing of heaven on their new government. At noon, two companies of colorful grenadiers marched to the Presidential mansion. One company—the tallest young men in town—was dressed in blue jackets faced with red and laced with gold, with white feathers in their cocked hats. The other, or German company, wore towering cone-shaped caps faced with black bear skin, and blue coats with yellow waistcoats. Gentlemen in carriages and citizens on foot had gathered with members of Congress who formed the official escort for the President.

Washington stepped into the state coach, drawn by four horses, and the full procession left for Federal Hall. There the military formed ranks, on each side of the street, through which Washington passed on his way to the Senate Chamber. He advanced between Senators and Representatives, bowing to each, and was conducted to the chair by Vice President Adams.

Later, while Washington made his inaugural address before Congress, the people poured into taverns and public houses and milled through the streets, with a warm air of camaraderie among all, to pass the time until dark. Then the city became a brilliant scene with splendid illuminations of the French and Spanish ambassadors' residences and public buildings. The *Carolina* in the harbor at sunset fired thirteen cannon and later in the evening looked like a glittering pyramid of stars.

From Chancellor Livingston's house, the President watched the fireworks that were set off from Fort George. A flight of thirteen rockets and the thundering of thirteen cannon both began and ended the brilliant pyrotechnical display. Between the Fort and Bowling Green, on Manhattan Island, was erected an enormous brilliant transparent portrait of the President. On his right hand was a figure of Justice, representing the Senate of the United States, and on his left hand Wisdom, representing the House of Representatives. High over the President's head was the American Eagle, supported by two gaily colored female figures.

At ten o'clock, the President walked back to his residence from Chancellor Livingston's, for the people thronged the streets so densely that no carriage could pass through. The extraordinary day at last drew to a close and *The Maryland Gazette* noted: "Every honest man must feel a singular felicity in contemplating this day—good government, the best of blessings, now commences under favorable auspices. We beg leave to congratulate our readers on the great event."

The inauguration ball had been postponed so that Mrs. Washington might attend, but, when the President's lady was further detained in Virginia, the brilliant ball was given on Thursday, May 5, in the City Assembly Rooms, a large wooden building at 115 Broadway. The splendid affair lasted until two o'clock. The President led out two cotillions and

The first inauguration ball, when Washington danced a stately minuet and led out two cotillions, was depicted by artist H. A. Ogden to grace the cover of Harper's Bazar *during the centennial celebration, in 1889, of the first inauguration.*

HARPER'S BAZAR.
A Repository of Fashion, Pleasure, and Instruction

Vol. XXII.—No. 19.
Copyright, 1889, by Harper & Brothers
All Rights Reserved

NEW YORK, SATURDAY, MAY 11, 1889.

TEN CENTS A COPY.
WITH SUPPLEMENTS.

danced a stately minuet that was, an observer noted, "well suited to his impressive dignity and courtliness."

In sharp contrast to the first inauguration, Washington's second inauguration on March 4, 1793, was a model of stark simplicity. The Federal government had moved to Philadelphia temporarily, while the new Federal City on the Potomac was being planned.

A few minutes before noon, Washington's handsome cream-colored coach, with cherubs painted on the door panels and drawn by six horses, rolled up to Congress Hall, a stone's throw from Independence Hall. Out stepped the President, dressed in a handsome black velvet suit trimmed with silver lace. An embroidered white satin vest, black silk stockings, low black shoes, diamond-studded knee and shoe buckles, yellow kid gloves, cocked hat and a dress sword with a jeweled hilt sheathed in a white leather scabbard completed his elegant attire.

This clay bust of George Washington was modeled from life by French sculptor Jean Antoine Houdon at Mount Vernon, where it is now on display in the museum.

At twelve o'clock precisely, the President entered the Senate Chamber on the second floor where the members of the Senate and the House of Representatives, Cabinet officers, the Judges of the Supreme Court and other government officers, the foreign ministers and a number of private Philadelphia citizens, both ladies and gentlemen, awaited.

Vice President Adams, who had also been re-elected to his post, was not present. He had gone to the bedside of his wife, who was ill in Massachusetts.

In Adams's absence, the President pro tempore of the Senate, John Langdon, greeted the President of the United States and said: "Sir, one of the Judges of the Supreme Court of the United States is now present and ready to administer to you the oath required by the Constitution, to be taken by the President of the United States."

The President first gave a concise and comprehensive speech consisting of 135 words—the shortest inaugural address on record. Then Supreme Court Judge William Cushing solemnly read the oath which the President repeated, phrase by phrase.

The President left the hall as quickly as he had come, without pomp or ceremony, and as he departed the people saluted him with three cheers. In the evening, the Dancing Assembly gave a ball which the President and Mrs. Washington attended.

JOHN ADAMS

☆　☆　☆

March 4, 1797

When John Adams, a Federalist, was inaugurated as the second President of the United States on March 4, 1797, in Philadelphia, he had won the election over two formidable contenders, Thomas Jefferson and Alexander Hamilton. Jefferson received the second highest number of electoral votes and became Vice President, even though he led the opposition, the Democratic-Republican party. At that time, each elector who had been chosen by his own state could cast, or withhold, his vote as he wished.

Soon after his election was declared, Adams sent the notification to both Houses of Congress, asking them to attend the inaugural ceremony at noon, the fourth of March, in the chamber of the House of Representatives which occupied the ground floor of Congress Hall. Spectators and official guests crowded into every square foot of space to witness the historic event when, in Adams's words, "The sight of the sun setting full orbed and another rising less splendid was a novelty."

Adams was noted for his integrity and independence, though his stern and frequently successful stand on controversial issues had not added to his personal popularity. One of the patriotic architects of independence, by profession he had been a schoolteacher, a lawyer, and a farmer, and also had served his country as a minister abroad. He once allowed that if family pride were excusable, "I should think a descent from a line of virtuous, independent New England farmers for a hundred and sixty years was a better foundation for it than a descent through royal and noble scoundrels ever since the flood."

With his election to the highest office in the land, Adams managed to

A rare engraving by Amos Doolittle shows John Adams surrounded by the crests of the sixteen United States.

justify to himself a departure from his normal frugal ways ingrained by his Puritan background. He ordered a new "chariot . . . simple but elegant enough," he wrote Mrs. Adams, and rode in it for the first time to his own inauguration. Abigail Smith Adams was in Braintree at the time, caring for his 88-year-old mother who died a month later.

When the 61-year-old President-elect, who had not slept well the night before, entered the hall, an outburst of spontaneous applause greeted him. An ovation also welcomed both President Washington and the new Vice President. Jefferson had taken the oath of office as Vice President of the United States at eleven o'clock in the Senate Chamber, where he gave a brief address.

Adams, who was five feet seven, took his seat on the elevated chair of the Speaker of the House with the two tall Virginians, Washington and Jefferson, and the Secretary of the Senate on his right. The Speaker and Clerk of the House were on his left and, at a table in the center, all the Supreme Court Judges.

The President-elect then arose and delivered his inaugural address in which, so he wrote Abigail, he was "determined to say some things as an appeal to Posterity," that, he declared, "foreign nations and future times will understand . . . better than my enemies or friends will own they do." At the conclusion, Adams stepped down to meet Chief Justice Oliver Ellsworth, who energetically administered the constitutional oath.

After repeating the oath, President Adams again sat down and surveyed the scene before him. He later reported that "there was more weeping than there has ever been at the Representation of any Tragedy." To many, it was the last occasion to see their beloved Washington, and the tears flowed profusely. For Adams, who was overshadowed by his predecessor in prestige and popularity, as well as height, it was a trying but memorable day.

"A Solemn Scene it was indeed," the President wrote to his wife, "and it was made more affecting to me by the presence of the General, whose countenance was as serene and unclouded as the day. He seem'd to me to enjoy a triumph over me. Methought I heard him think ay! I am fairly out and you fairly in! See which of us will be the happiest."

After a few moments the new President rose, bowed to the audience, and left the hall. Vice President Jefferson and General Washington followed, after conducting a bowing contest with respect to precedence. Washington declared that the new Vice President now outranked him and insisted that Jefferson lead the way and the new Vice President, with great reluctance, consented.

The President was escorted to his temporary residence by Vice President Jefferson and there Washington called on him to congratulate him, wishing his administration to be happy, successful, and honorable. In the

John Adams's manuscript of his inaugural address, written in a copybook now preserved in the National Archives, shows the President's changes in his original text.

The corner of Sixth and Chestnut streets in Philadelphia changed little, except for the people's dress, from the eighteenth century until Ferdinand Reichardt painted "Philadelphia in 1858." Congress Hall, the site of Washington's second inauguration and of John Adams's inauguration, is at right, with the steeple of Independence Hall at left center.

evening the merchants of Philadelphia gave a banquet in honor not of Adams but of Washington. Leftovers from the feast were sent to the jail and to the sick in the hospital.

But much as he fussed, Adams conceded to his wife that "what they call the Inauguration" was, all agreed, "the sublimest Thing ever exhibited in America." This contemporary account, from a newsletter written by Robert Goodloe Harper, a member of the House of Representatives from South Carolina, to his constituents confirms that view:

"It was certainly an interesting spectacle to see the Chief Magistrate of a great people descend voluntarily from his station, and join his fellow citizens in attending at the elevation of his successor; to see that successor assume amidst the congratulations even of his opposers, the station to which the voice of his fellow-citizens had raised him; to see the two distinguished citizens who lately were rival candidates for the highest office, cheerfully submit to the decision of the majority and unite with cordiality in serving their country, each in the post which their country had assigned to them! These circumstances form the highest encomium of republican government, and on the character of our country, and they furnish additional grounds for the pleasing confidence, that our constitution will disappoint, by its durability and happy effects, the predictions of its enemies, and the fears of its friends."

THOMAS JEFFERSON

☆ ☆ ☆

March 4, 1801   March 4, 1805

The first inauguration in the new capital city of Washington was held on March 4, 1801, when Thomas Jefferson took the oath of office as third President of the United States. However, up until two weeks before the inauguration, a threatening cloud had hung over the country because the outcome of the presidential election was uncertain. There had been a tie between Thomas Jefferson and Aaron Burr, both Democratic-Republicans. The Federalist President John Adams had lost the election after only one term in office.

The tie in the votes had thrown the election of the President into the House of Representatives where, according to the Constitution, each state could cast one vote. The House met in a dramatic session that lasted thirty hours, only two weeks before the inaugural day, and, while a tremendous mob milled around the Capitol, the tie was finally broken by a single vote. Thomas Jefferson of Virginia was declared duly elected as the President of the United States, with Aaron Burr of New York as Vice President. The decision was accepted, and the threat of violence and anarchy from the Burr faction quickly dissipated.

Early in the morning of Wednesday, March 4, a salute by the Washington artillery thundered through the new Federal city. Only one wing of the Capitol building, the Senate, had been completed, and the President's house, a mile away, was still unfinished. Linking these two stately, white-stone edifices that were rising in the wilderness was, according to L'Enfant's plan, a grand avenue. But, in 1801, Pennsylvania Avenue was still a wide, muddy path of ruts hacked through trees, brush, and swamp grass.

Thomas Jefferson. A drawing by Benjamin Henry Latrobe about 1801.

The President-elect, a widower, had lodgings at Conrad and McMunn's boardinghouse on New Jersey Avenue, a short walk from the Capitol. He had resigned as President of the Senate a few days before his inauguration. Jefferson knew that President Adams was leaving seven horses and two carriages, all the property of the United States, in the stables of the President's household for his use, but on his inauguration day he preferred to walk, true to his "leveling principles" of democracy.

About ten o'clock the Alexandria company of riflemen and a company of artillery paraded in front of Jefferson's boardinghouse. Two hours later the 57-year-old President-elect came out and walked over to the Capitol, escorted by many members of Congress and his fellow citizens.

He stood out in a crowd, for he was a tall man, six feet two, with a freckled face and gray, neglected hair that still had traces of the sandy red mane he had had when he drafted the Declaration of Independence twenty-five years before. He could, when he chose, be an elegant, dashing figure, but the costume he wore on his inauguration day was described as a blue coat, a gray hairy waistcoat, red under-waistcoat, green velveteen breeches, and gray yarn stockings.

In addition to notifying the presiding officers of both Houses of Congress of his forthcoming inauguration plans, Jefferson had written to John Marshall, the new Chief Justice and acting Secretary of State, ask-

16

ing him to administer the oath and also to see if the oath prescribed in the Constitution was the only one necessary for Jefferson to take. Marshall replied that he would, with pleasure, administer the oath and promised to be punctual, but added that he could find no information regarding the oaths Jefferson's presidential predecessors had taken. "That prescribed in the constitution seems to me to be the only one which is to be administered," Marshall wrote.

Jefferson's entrance into the Capitol was announced by another volley of artillery, and as he strode into the Senate Chamber the members of both Houses of Congress stood up, Vice President Burr relinquished the chair to the President-elect, and Jefferson sat down for a few moments. Then he rose, and in a tone so low that few heard it, delivered his inaugural speech in the semi-circular chamber crowded by nearly a thousand persons.

Jefferson again sat down briefly after his address, then walked over to the clerk's table where Chief Justice Marshall administered the oath. The brief ceremony over, the artillery signaled the President's departure.

The President then walked back to his lodgings accompanied by Vice President Burr, the Chief Justice, the heads of departments, and the chief clerk of the State Department, who was being loaned to the new President until a private secretary could be provided. Jefferson received the citizens who called on him and then, to the distress of his fellow boarders, insisted on taking his old seat at the foot of the table—the far-

The Senate wing of the Capitol, shown in this watercolor by W. R. Birch, was the only part of the Capitol completed at Jefferson's inauguration there in 1801.

SPEECH
Of Mr. *Jefferson* at his
Inauguration.

WASHINGTON, March 4.

President's Speech.

THIS DAY
At Twelve O'Clock,
THOMAS JEFFERSON,
President of the United States.

Took the oath of office required by the Constitution, in the Senate Chamber, in the presence of the Senate, the Members of the House of Representatives, the Public Officers, and a large concourse of Citizens.

Previously to which he delivered the following

ADDRESS.
Friends and Fellow Citizens,

Called upon to undertake the duties of the first executive office of our country, I avail myself of the presence of that portion of my fellow citizens which is here assembled, to express my grateful thanks for the favour with which they have been pleased to look towards me, to declare a sincere consciousness that the task is above my talents, and that I approach it with those anxious and awful presentiments that the greatness of the charge, and the weakness of my powers so justly inspire. A rising nation, spread over a wide and fruitful land, traversing all the seas with the rich productions of their industry, engaged in commerce with nations who feel power and forget right, advancing rapidly to destinies beyond the reach of mortal eye; when I contemplate these transcendent objects and see the honour, the happiness, and the hopes of this beloved country committed to the issue and the auspices of this day, I shrink from the contemplation, and humble myself before the magnitude of the undertaking. Utterly indeed should I despair, did not the presence of many, whom I here see, remind me, that in the other high authorities provided by our constitution, I shall find resources of wisdom, of virtue, and of zeal, on which to rely under all difficulties. To you, then, gentlemen, who are charged with the sovereign functions of the legislation, and to those associated with you, I look with encouragement for that guidance and support which may enable us to steer with safety the vessel in which we are all embarked, amidst the conflicting elements of a troubled world.

During the contest of opinion through which we have past, the animation of discussions and of exertions has sometimes worn an aspect which might impose on strangers unused to think freely, and to speak and to write what they think : but this being now decided by the voice of the nation, announced according to the rules of the constitution, all will of course arrange themselves under the will of the law, and unite in common efforts for the common good. All too will bear in mind this sacred principle, that though the will of the majority is in all cases to prevail, that will to be rightful must be reasonable ; that the minority possess their equal rights, which equal laws must protect, and to violate would be oppression. Let us then, fellow citizens, unite with one heart and and mind, let us restore to social intercourse that harmony and affection without which liberty and even life itself, are but dreary things. And let us reflect that having banished from our land that religious intolerance under which mankind so long bled and suffered, we have yet gained little, if we countenance a political intolerance as despotic, as wicked, and capable of as bitter and bloody persecutions. During the throes and convulsions of the ancient world; during the agonizing spasms of infuriate man, seeking through blood and slaughter his long lost liberty, it was not wonderful that the agitation of the billows should reach even this distant and peaceful shore : that this should be more felt and feared by some and less by others ; and should divide opinions as to measures of safety ; but every difference of opinion is not a difference of principle. We have called by different names brethren of the same principle. We are all REPUBLICANS: We are all FEDERALISTS. If there be any among us who would wish to dissolve this union or to change its republican form, let them stand undisturbed as monuments of the safety with which error of opinion may be tolerated, where reason is left free to combat it. I know indeed that some honest men fear that a republican government cannot be strong enough. But would the honest patriot, in the full tide of successful experiment, abandon a government which has so far kept us free and firm, on the theoretic and visionary fear, that this government, the world's best hope, may, by possibility, want energy to preserve itself ? I trust not. I believe this, on the contrary, the strongest government on earth. I believe it the one, where every man, at the call of the law, would fly to the standard of the law, and would meet invasions of the public order as his own personal concern—Sometimes it is said that man cannot be trusted with the government of himself. Can he then be trusted with the government of others ? Or have we found angels in the form of kings to govern him ? Let history answer this question.

Let us then, with courage and confidence, pursue our own federal and republican principles : our attachment to union and representative government. Kindly separated by nature and a wide ocean from the exterminating havoc of one quarter of the globe ; too high minded to endure the degradations of the others, possessing a chosen country, with room enough for our descendants to the thousandth and thousandth generation, entertaining a due sense of our equal right to the use of our own faculties, to the acquisitions of our own industry, to honor and confidence from our fellow citizens, resulting not from birth, but from our actions and their sense of them, enlightened by a benign religion, professed indeed and practised in various forms, yet all of them inculcating honesty, truth, temperance, gratitude and the love of man, acknowledging and adorning an overruling Providence, which by all its dispensations proves that it delights in the happiness of man here, and his greatest happiness hereafter ; with all these blessings, what more is necessary to make us a happy and a prosperous people? Still one thing more, fellow-citizens, a wise and frugal government, which shall restrain men from injuring one another, shall leave them otherwise free to regulate their own pursuits of industry and improvement, and shall not take from the mouth of labor the bread it has earned. This is the sum of good government ; and this is necessary to close the circle of our felicities.

About to enter, fellow citizens, on the exercise of duties which comprehend every thing dear and valuable to you, it is proper you should understand what I deem the essential principles of our government, and consequently those which ought to shape its administration. I will compress them within the narrowest compass they will bear, stating the general principle, but not all its limitations. Equal and exact justice to all men, of whatever state or persuasion, religious or political :—peace, commerce and honest friendship with all nations, entangling alliances with none :—the support of the state governments in all their rights, as the most competent administrations for our domestic concerns, and the surest bulwarks against anti-republican tendencies :—the preservation of the general government in its whole constitutional vigour, as the sheet anchor of our peace at home, and safety abroad :—a jealous care of the right of election by the people, a mild and safe corrective of abuses which are lopped by the sword of revolution where peaceable remedies are unprovided :—absolute acquiescence in the decisions of the majority, the vital principle of republics, from which is no appeal but to force, the vital principle and immediate parent of despotism :—a well disciplined militia, our best reliance in peace, and for the first moments of war, till regulars may relieve them :—the supremacy in the public expence, that labor may be lightly burthened :—the honest payment of our debts and sacred preservation of the public faith :—encouragement of agriculture, and of commerce as its hand-maid :—the diffusion of information, and arraignment of all abuses at the bar of the public reason :—freedom of religion; freedom of the press; and freedom of person, under the protection of the Habeas Corpus :—and trial by juries impartially selected. These principles form the bright constellation, which has gone before us, and guided our steps through an age of revolution and information. They should be the creed of our political faith, the text of civic instruction ; the touch-stone by which to try the services of those we trust ; and should we wander from them in moments of error or of alarm, let us hasten to retrace our steps, and to regain the road which alone leads to peace, liberty and safety.

I repair, then, fellow-citizens, to the post you have assigned me. With experience enough in subordinate offices to have seen the difficulties of this the greatest of all, I have learnt to expect that it will rarely fall to the lot of imperfect man to retire from this station with the reputation, and the favor, which bring him into it. Without pretensions to that confidence which you reposed in our first and greatest revolutionary character, whose pre-eminent services had entitled him to the first place in his country's love, and destined for him the fairest page in the volume of faithful history. I ask so much confidence only, as may give firmness and effect to the legal administration of our affairs. I shall often go wrong through defect of judgment. When right, I shall often be thought wrong by those whose positions will not command a view of the whole ground. I ask your indulgence for my own errors, which will never be intentional ; and your support against the errors of others, who may condemn what they would not if seen in all its parts. The approbation implied by your suffrage, is a great consolation to me for the past ; and my future solicitude will be, to retain the good opinion of those who have bestowed it in advance, to conciliate that of others, by doing them all the good in my power, and to be instrumental to the happiness and freedom of all.

Relying then on the patronage of your good will, I advance with obedience to the work, ready to retire from it whenever you become sensible how much better choices it is in your power to make. And may that infinite power, which leads our councils to what is best, and give them a favourable issue for your peace and prosperity.

thest away from the fire—at a dinner attended by civic and military leaders. The city was in a festive mood and many citizens from adjacent counties had come to town to celebrate, too. At night there was a "pretty general illumination" throughout the city.

Retiring President Adams was not at the inaugural ceremony. The Republican newspaper, which had favored Jefferson during election, announced that Adams had "left the city at daylight," and Adams's political foes made the most of it. However, an exchange of letters in March between the two splendid but dissimilar old patriots indicates there was no slight received, and none intended, by Adams's quiet departure from the capital. Futhermore, Jefferson had dined with the President and Mrs. Adams in the new, unfinished President's house on Pennsylvania Avenue after Adams's political defeat, which was certainly a bitter disappointment to the President. But though their longstanding friendship had, indeed, been sorely strained by the virulence of the political battle, Adams was relieved when Jefferson prevailed in the final voting, for he could not tolerate Burr.

Both Jefferson and Adams knew that Adams had been overshadowed by his predecessor at his own inauguration, and there is no evidence that Adams was invited to take part in his successor's inauguration. Furthermore, Adams was mourning for his son, Charles, whose death had coincided with Adams's political defeat. From Stonyfield, his home in Quincy (Braintree), Adams wrote to Jefferson on March 24, 1801:

"This part of the union is in a state of perfect tranquility & I see nothing to obscure your prospect of a quiet & prosperous administration which I heartily wish you."

The former President was now Farmer John of Stonyfield. The era of Mr. Jefferson's democratic republic had begun.

Four years later, less attention was given to Jefferson's second inaugural day when both the President and a new Vice President, George Clinton, were sworn into office.

As the throng streamed out of the Capitol on March 4, 1801, copies of the inaugural speech were being distributed. Early that morning Jefferson had given a copy of his speech to Samuel Harrison Smith, his good friend and editor of the Republican newspaper, The National Intelligencer. *Smith had the speech printed immediately as a broadside, and with it scored the first "extra" in American newspaper history.*

A crude sketch of Thomas Jefferson appears on this mug, a souvenir of the first inauguration in Washington.

On a sunny Monday, March 4, 1805, Jefferson rode horseback, attended by his secretary and his groom, along the broad Pennsylvania Avenue that he had landscaped with two rows of Lombardy poplars on either side to the Capitol. There, dressed in black with silk stockings, Jefferson again delivered an inaudible inaugural speech in the Senate Chamber.

Augustus John Foster, secretary of the British legation in Washington, later wrote home that the President "then kissed the book & swore before the Chief Justice to be faithful to the Constitution, then bowed & retired as before." Defeated Vice President Burr watched from the gallery.

John Quincy Adams, the son of former President Adams, walked the long mile to the President's house to pay his compliments to Jefferson. The British secretary, who had turned up in clothes and decorations suitable for a similar occasion at the court of St. James's, wrote home that all who chose attended the levee, "even towards the close blacks & dirty boys, who drank his wine & lolled upon his couches before us all—the jingling of a few fifes & drums finished the day. There was nothing dignified in the whole affair."

The most memorable event of the day had been a spontaneous procession that escorted Jefferson when he left the Capitol to return to the President's house. Mechanics from the navy yard marched to military music, displaying the insignia of their professions. It was the first inaugural parade ever seen on the long, wide Pennsylvania Avenue.

JAMES MADISON

☆ ☆ ☆

March 4, 1809   March 4, 1813

James Madison was inaugurated on Saturday, March 4, 1809, in the magnificent new chamber of the House of Representatives which had been in use more than a year. The 57-year-old Madison, who was Jefferson's Secretary of State and choice for his successor, had already spent over thirty years in service to his country.

"The great little Madison," as Aaron Burr called him, was a small man, about five feet four, who was once described as "no bigger than half a piece of soap." He had blue eyes, a ruddy face, a low voice, and modest ways. He was balding, wore a queue and powder, and walked with a quick, bouncing step.

Madison was one of the most brilliant and remarkable men who participated in the birth of the nation. His cool, logical legal arguments and eloquent way with words had made him the "Father of the Constitution," and it was Madison who drafted the first ten amendments—the Bill of Rights.

For days before the inauguration, people had been pouring into the city. One innkeeper on the road to Washington had seen three stage-coaches pass by in a single day! On the morning of his inauguration, Madison asked Jefferson to ride in his carriage to the Capitol. The retiring President declined because, he said, he didn't want "to divide the honors of the day." With his 17-year-old grandson, Thomas Jefferson Randolph, as his sole companion, the President rode horseback up the avenue from the President's house to the Capitol.

Shortly before noon on the brisk, brilliant day, Madison left his F Street house in his carriage, escorted by troops of cavalry from Washington and Georgetown. A procession of plain citizens, some in carriages, others on horseback, and more on foot, flocked after him to the Capitol where ten thousand people waited outside. The area allotted to citizens in the Representatives' Hall had been filled to overflowing for hours.

The President arrived at the Capitol at twelve and was ushered into the hall by a senatorial committee. Vice President Clinton, who had been re-elected, was not present, and the President pro tempore of the Senate, John Milledge, conducted Madison to the chair. A seat of honor near the new President had been reserved for the retiring one, which Jefferson declined with the explanation, "This day I return to the people and my proper seat is among them." Complained one observer, "Surely this was carrying democracy too far."

Madison wore clothes with a stylish flair and at his inauguration was dressed in a dark brown suit of American-grown Merino wool and American manufacture. He delivered a short speech with, *The Monitor*

James Madison, painted by John Vanderlyn

The new Representatives' wing of the Capitol, left, was the site of Madison's inauguration in 1809. This design, from the east, showing the Senate wing on the north at right, was published by Birch in 1807. The American eagle swooping protectively over the Capitol clutches the crest of the United States of North America in its talons.

noted, that distinctness and accuracy for which he was remarkable, but his tone of voice was so low that John Quincy Adams couldn't hear it. Then Chief Justice Marshall, in his Supreme Court robes, administered the oath.

Minute guns were fired to signal the conclusion of the ceremony and again when the President left the Capitol. He reviewed nine companies of infantry in full military uniform from the District of Columbia, then entered his carriage and returned home with the cavalry escort.

Dolley Madison, the first President's wife to see her husband inaugurated, hurried home to F Street where she had refreshments spread out for the well-wishers who immediately crowded the house. Many had to wait in the street for half an hour before they could get in.

The President stood near the door of the drawing room with his wife and greeted all with cordiality. Mrs. Madison had a smile for everyone and was, said a guest, "all dignity, grace and affability." She wore a plain cambric dress with a long train and a purple velvet bonnet trimmed with white satin and white plumes.

Jefferson, on horseback, followed the crowd to Madison's house, and *The Monitor*'s editor reported: "I saw this exalted man as he rode along the Pennsylvania Avenue, in his usual dress, like a common citizen. The sight of him at such a moment, was calculated to excite sensations of pleasing melancholy. This was the last public occasion when we should behold him in our city. . . ."

Later the crowd went on to the President's mansion—sometimes called "the white house"—on Pennsylvania Avenue to pay a farewell visit to Jefferson before he retired to his Virginia home, Monticello.

A grand inauguration ball was held in the evening at Long's Hotel, at First and A Streets, Southeast, and more than four hundred persons came to the gala event. Jefferson was among the first to arrive and was in high spirits as the band played "Jefferson's March." The chatty editor of *The Monitor* understood that it was "nearly 20 years since Mr. Jefferson was present at a dancing assembly. . . . A strong mark of respect for his enlightened successor."

Inauguration Ball.

Those gentlemen who are in the habit o attending the city assemblies, &c. are requested to meet at Long's Hotel on Monday evening next, about five o'clock, for the purpose of making arrangements for an inauguration ball.
February 25, 1809.

The first official inauguration ball was hastily arranged in response to this newspaper advertisement in The Monitor, *Saturday, February 25, 1809. Tickets for the ball became available at the bar of the ball site, Long's Hotel.*

The band struck up "President Madison's March" and Mrs. Madison made a grand entrance on the arm of one of the ball's managers, followed by her sister, Mrs. Richard Cutts, on the President's arm. People stood on benches to catch a glimpse of the President, who wore a black velvet suit with ruffles at the neck, his powdered queue tied with a black velvet ribbon. Dolley Madison wore a pale buff-colored velvet gown and pearls with a turban of matching velvet and white satin, trimmed with bird of

The United States Capitol, with a wooden walkway between the Senate wing (left) and the Representatives' wing, as seen from Pennsylvania Avenue at the west front of the Capitol, looked rather like this romanticized watercolor, attributed to Benjamin Henry Latrobe, at Madison's second inauguration on March 4, 1813.

paradise plumes. She thoroughly enjoyed the ball, but the President confided to a friend: "I would much rather be in bed."

Windows were smashed in the hot, crowded quarters to let in air when the sashes would not let down. Immediately after an elegant supper the President and Mrs. Madison left, but the dancing lasted until midnight when the music stopped as the clock struck the hour.

It was the first inauguration ball to be planned and held on the very day of the inauguration as part of the official ceremonies, and was a splendid way to close an exceptional day. But some agreed with John Quincy Adams: "The crowd was excessive, the heat oppressive, and the entertainment bad."

The young nation was at war with Great Britain when Madison took the presidential oath of office for the second time on March 4, 1813, but

The President's House looked like this during Madison's administration, about 1810. The eagle gateposts, stone wall, and fence, as well as the low, terrace-pavilions that flank either side, were built during Jefferson's administration from designs by Jefferson and Latrobe, who served as Surveyor of Public Buildings during the administrations of both Jefferson and Madison.

the battles of the War of 1812, being mainly fought at sea, seemed far from the capital.

The ceremonies were remarkably similar to the scene of four years before. At the Capitol the new Vice President, Elbridge Gerry, presided in the House of Representatives where both Houses of Congress had gathered. Following the President's address, the oath was again administered by Chief Justice Marshall and Madison was escorted back to the President's house. The multitude arrived on his heels to eat his ice cream and bonbons and drink his Madeira, reported the wife of newspaper editor William W. Seaton, "for every creature that could afford twenty-five cents for hack-hire was present."

In the evening the President and Mrs. Madison graced the festive ball, a lively affair at Davis's Hotel on Pennsylvania Avenue near Sixth Street, with their presence. No doubt the President concealed a yawn and slipped off for home and bed as early as decorum would allow, but the inauguration ball was firmly established as the popular and traditional way to bring the inauguration day to a close.

JAMES MONROE

☆ ☆ ☆

March 4, 1817   March 5, 1821

On March 1, 1817, when James Monroe wrote to John Gaillard, the acting President of the Senate, asking him "to inform the Honorable Senate of the United States" that he planned to take the presidential oath of office "on Tuesday, the 4th inst., at 12 o'clock in the chamber of the House of Representatives," he had no idea of the storm that would ensue. The Representatives' Chamber was on the second floor of Congress Hall, or the "little Brick Capitol," which had been built as a temporary meeting place for Congress at the corner of First and A Streets, a block from the skeleton of the Capitol that had been burned by the British in August, 1814.

The Senate committee for inauguration arrangements decided to place the fine, red chairs from the Senate Chamber, located on the first floor, in the Representatives' Chamber upstairs. But the committee made a tactless error. Only as an afterthought did they ask Speaker of the House Henry Clay for permission to use the Representatives' Chamber. Clay not only objected to substituting the Senate's fancy red chairs for the "plain democratic chairs" in the House but, he said, he feared for the safety of the building if a crowd were to congregate on the second floor. So a temporary portico was erected outdoors at the front of the hall especially for the inaugural ceremony. The little Brick Capitol survived for more than a century but had to be knocked down to make way for the new Supreme Court Building.

The arrangements for this unique inauguration started traditions in inaugural ceremonies that became firmly established years later. For this was the first presidential inauguration held outdoors in Washington, the

27

This portrait of James Monroe by Rembrandt Peale now hangs in the James Monroe Museum and Memorial Library, where he once practised law, in Fredericksburg, Virginia.

first ever to take place on an inaugural platform erected specifically for the occasion, and the first at which the President made his inaugural address to the multitude.

March 4 was a radiantly mild spring day and the President-elect set out from his residence at 2017 I Street about half-past eleven. A cavalcade of citizens on horseback, responding to a public notice signed by the mayors of Georgetown and Washington—the inaugural committee of the day—formed the escort that clattered along behind Monroe's carriage, arriving at Congress Hall a little before noon.

The tall, slender 58-year-old man who stepped from his carriage was greeted with military honors by the Marine Corps, the Georgetown Riflemen, and artillery and infantry from Alexandria. Monroe had left William and Mary College at the age of eighteen to join the Continental Army, and he still dressed in the old style. He habitually wore a cutaway coat with a lace stock at the neck, and tight knee britches—smallclothes—and shoes with buckles. A frank, honest expression in his blue eyes inspired confidence in keeping with Jefferson's remark that Monroe was so honest "if you turned his soul inside out there would not be a spot on it."

Arriving at the same time were President Madison and the Supreme Court Judges. All entered the Senate, where Vice President-elect Daniel Tompkins was sworn into office. Then the entire body escorted the

President and President-elect to the elevated portico outdoors. There, under brilliant skies, Monroe rose and delivered his inaugural speech to an immense gathering of between five and eight thousand Congressmen, foreign representatives, strangers, and citizens—"ladies as well as gentlemen," it was noted by the press. Chief Justice Marshall, Monroe's former classmate at William and Mary, then administered the oath which was announced by a single gun, followed by artillery salutes from near and far—the Navy Yard, the battery, and Fort Warburton.

"The ceremony and the spectacle were simple, but grand, animating and impressive," *The National Intelligencer* told its readers the next day, and also noted chattily, "we heard of no accident during the day, notwithstanding the magnitude of the assemblage."

The President again took the salute on his departure and was escorted home. With his wife, Elizabeth, he received "the visits" of foreign diplomats and members of the United States government, "of strangers and citizens." The well-wishers later went on to call on former President and Mrs. Madison.

The Old Brick Capitol, site of Monroe's first inauguration in 1817, was being used as a prison during the Civil War when this photograph was taken by Matthew Brady or one of his assistants.

The new President and James Madison and their ladies were present at the gala ball at Davis's Hotel in the evening. The administration of James Monroe had commenced with a long and glorious day.

For the first time in the young nation's existence, the traditional date for the President's inauguration, the fourth of March, fell on Sunday in 1821, the beginning of Monroe's second term. Chief Justice Marshall advised that the inauguration be held on Monday, March 5, and the country was, technically, without a President for a day.

At Monroe's request, his Cabinet officers assembled at the President's house where, together with the Marshal of the District Tench Ringgold and his deputy, they made up the President's only escort. The President wore a full suit of black broadcloth "of somewhat antiquated fashion," noted Secretary of State John Quincy Adams, with shoe and hose buckles, and "rode in a plain carriage with four horses and a single colored footman." The Secretaries of State, Treasury, War, and the Navy, each in a carriage drawn by a pair of horses, followed along deserted Pennsylvania Avenue, for there had been heavy rain and snowfall during the night. By contrast, the halls at the rebuilt Capitol were choked with people. It took the President and his Cabinet several minutes to press their way through the mass of humanity into the Representatives' Chamber, and the British Minister, Sir Stratford Canning, in full court dress, was among those left outside in the throng.

At the entrance of the President, the music of the Marine Band enlivened the scene in the chamber, packed wall to wall with more than two thousand people, the seats occupied by ladies. The President took a seat in front of the Speaker's chair with Chief Justice Marshall on his right. They stood and, as the Chief Justice merely held the book, the President repeated the constitutional oath. Then the Chief Justice remained standing by his side while the President delivered his address, despite considerable commotion in the gallery. At its conclusion, several persons shook hands with the President, who then departed as the Marine Band played and a cheering shout went up from the galleries.

At the President's house, which the Monroes had occupied since its renovation after the war, the President received congratulations of visitors. Monroe and his family attended the gala ball that evening at Brown's Indian Queen Hotel on Pennsylvania Avenue but left before supper, as reported by the Secretary of State, who "finished a fatiguing and bustling day about midnight."

JOHN QUINCY ADAMS

☆ ☆ ☆

March 4, 1825

John Quincy Adams, the only son of a President to become President of the United States, was elected by the House of Representatives. The younger Adams, whose venerable father, John Adams, was too old, at ninety, to come to his son's inauguration on March 4, 1825, had at fifty-seven a lifetime of public service both behind and ahead of him. But the votes in the presidential election had been split among five candidates so that no one received a majority of electoral votes, as prescribed by the Constitution, and the election was thrown into the House of Representatives for the second time in twenty-four years. There the members voted on the three highest candidates. When defeated Henry Clay threw his support to Adams, the latter was declared duly elected President, to the everlasting bitterness of Andrew Jackson of Tennessee, who had polled the highest number of both popular and electoral votes.

Adam's inauguration on a cloudy day turned out to be the most impressive demonstration seen in Washington to date. People had been streaming into the capital for five days, and by nine o'clock on the inaugural morning crowds were clamoring at the doors of the Capitol. Men escorting ladies, who were "allowed the privilege of their sex in being admitted to seats," had to fight their way to the doors.

The President-elect had spent two sleepless nights at his F Street home. Louisa Catherine Adams had been extremely ill and on that very morning her husband summoned Dr. Henry Huntt to attend her. Then about midnight on the eve of the inauguration, proof copy of the inaugural address had arrived from *The National Intelligencer*, which Adams promptly corrected and returned.

John Quincy Adams: Left, *inaugural medal;* Right, *contemporary French lithograph by H. Brunet.*

Monroe's carriage arrived about 11:30 A.M. in front of Adams's home, where the militia and volunteer companies of the District, in full uniform, had gathered. Then, with the cavalry leading the way, the President's carriage followed that of his successor to the Capitol in a handsome procession, with a cavalcade of citizens, and music by several corps. The Marine Corps, stationed in line in front of the Capitol, saluted the President with music on his entrance into the building.

At twenty minutes past twelve, the citizen marshals, wearing blue scarfs, entered the Representatives' Hall, followed by the officers of both Houses of Congress and the President-elect, who shortly before had watched Vice President John C. Calhoun take the oath of office in the Senate Chamber. Then came the venerable President Monroe with his family, followed in procession by the black-robed Supreme Court Judges, the Vice President, and many members of both the Senate and House.

Adams, who was known to be plain, unassuming, and unostentatious though he had served his country as minister at foreign courts since he was twenty-seven years old, was five feet seven and wore a plain black broadcloth suit, with long trousers, of American manufacture. He took his seat in the elevated Speaker's chair and once silence prevailed in the galleries he rose and clearly read a forty-minute address, which evoked applause first from the galleries, then throughout the whole assembly. He stepped down to the Clerk's table, where the Supreme Court Judges were seated, and "received from the Chief Justice, a volume of the laws of the United States, from which he read, in a loud and clear voice, the oath of office," reported *The National Intelligencer*. Applause mingled with cheers arose in the galleries, immediately followed by the booming of artillery.

There was a moving exchange of congratulations and greeting between the new President and "his venerated predecessor," and, as congratulations poured in, among the first to shake his hand was General Jackson. The President was escorted back to his residence where Mrs. Adams, despite her illness, received in the drawing room and the President greeted both friends and strangers with his usual cordiality and unaffected manners. The President then called on the former President and Mrs. Monroe in "the mansion" and returned home for dinner. That rainy evening he went, without his ailing wife, to the ball at Carusi's Saloon, at the corner of Eleventh Street and Pennsylvania Avenue, where in the spacious hall crescent-shaped staircases led up to the entrance, on either side of which was a large fireplace heaped with blazing logs. Former President Monroe also attended the celebration in honor of his former Secretary of State, the new President.

At the end of the inaugural day, President Adams concluded in his diary: "I closed the day as it had begun, with Thanksgivings to God for all His mercies and favors past, and with prayers for the continuance of them to my country, and to myself and mine."

The President's House during the John Quincy Adams administration, depicted in this aquatint by Henry Stone in 1825, published by H & J. Stone, Washington, 1826.

ANDREW JACKSON

☆ ☆ ☆

March 4, 1829   March 4, 1833

While Andrew Jackson was being inaugurated as President on Ash Wednesday, March 4, 1829, John Quincy Adams went horseback riding. "Old Hickory," as Jackson's loyal troops had nicknamed him during the War of 1812, had at last won over his old opponent in a bitter political campaign. The President-elect, wearing a ten-inch black crepe mourning band on his hat for his beloved wife Rachel, had settled in at Gadsby's Hotel three weeks before the inauguration and arrived (so he told the Postmaster General) with the intention of paying the customary call on President Adams but was dissuaded from it by his friends. The insult to the President was the talk of the town. Commented one newspaper editor: "It was such a mark of indiginity that self-respect forbids Mr. Adams to overlook it."

The President, though stung, was determined to carry out the courtesies of the occasion. He sent word to Jackson that he would leave the President's house so that Jackson might "receive his visits of congratulations" there. Jackson sent his thanks to the President and said that if it were inconvenient, not to hurry. There was not a word about a place for the President in the inaugural ceremonies. Adams rented a house on Meridian Hill, north of the city, and put a notice in the newspapers requesting the citizens who might plan to call on him, as was the custom, "to dispense with that formality." Adams consulted with his Cabinet members, more affronted than he by the indignity shown him, and they were against his attending the inaugural ceremonies the next day.

For Jackson, the Hero of New Orleans, the fruits of political victory had lost their sweetness soon after the election when his wife died as

Andrew Jackson, painted by Ralph E. W. Earl.

Below: *Artist Howard Pyle's conception of President-elect Jackson on his way to Washington in 1829 was published in* Harper's Weekly *in 1881.*

English toile showing portraits of the United States Presidents commemorates the first inauguration of Jackson, March 4, 1829.

they were preparing to leave their Tennessee home for the nation's capital. The triumphal tour became a sad journey for Jackson, who was accompanied by his adopted family on the long trip from The Hermitage, near Nashville. The party traveled by flatboat and the steamboat *Pennsylvania* up the Mississippi and Ohio Rivers to Louisville, Cincinnati, and Pittsburgh, then overland by stagecoach to Washington. Everywhere the crowds swarmed to greet him and shake his hand, for Jackson was the People's Choice, the first frontiersman elevated to the highest office in the growing nation. Soon he complained of an aching right hand to add to his other pains, for the 61-year-old general carried an old lung wound from a duel.

"People have come from five hundred miles to see General Jackson, and they really seem to think that the country is rescued from some

36

dreadful danger," Daniel Webster wrote from Washington. The multitude, estimated as high as thirty thousand, filled the city and spilled over into the taverns and boardinghouses of Georgetown and Alexandria.

Firing early in the morning signaled the inaugural day but General Jackson, in deep mourning, had banned a military escort or a magnificent parade and even refused a carriage made of hickory wood offered by Baltimore citizens. He preferred to walk to the Capitol, he said, and wore a suit of plain black cloth made by enterprising citizens of Baltimore. But Jackson could not resist a group of fifteen gallant old Revo-

Wood engraving of Jackson's first inaugural address, printed on satin, is a treasured keepsake. This one, in its original frame with blown glass cover, now hangs in Jackson's home, The Hermitage, near Nashville, Tennessee.

lutionary officers and soldiers who had fought under Washington. They marched in procession to Gadsby's and solicited the honor of forming his escort. "Our advanced ages preclude the idea that this is designed to be a military pageant," they slyly added.

With the old soldiers and his comrades in arms from the Battle of New Orleans, the tall, lean old warrior strode up Pennsylvania Avenue, his white hair stirring in the gentle spring breeze above the heads in the the crowd as he acknowledged the salutations of the people who flocked along the way to the Capitol. His harsh, gaunt features were marked by the dignity of a gentleman and a soldier. The old General climbed over a parapet and entered the Capitol by the west basement door, for the dense mass of colorful humanity swarmed among the marble pillars on the East Portico and the grand steps. A ship's cable stretched across the steps kept them back from the elevated platform, erected for the inaugural ceremonies. A rending shout announced the General's arrival on the platform, and, with a dignified, sweeping bow, he commenced his inaugural address. He wore two sets of spectacles—one for reading the speech, the other—perched on top of his head—for viewing the

The "President's Levee or all Creation going to the White House, Washington," is the title of English artist Robert Cruickshank's aquatint depicting Jackson's first inaugural reception.

The inaugural ball gown of Emily Donelson, who acted as First Lady of the White House for the widower President Jackson, her uncle, is the earliest inaugural gown now on display in the First Ladies Hall of the Smithsonian Institution. Mrs. Donelson chose a dress of gold brocaded satin, complementing her titian hair, for the inaugural ball in 1829.

crowd. Shortly before Vice President Calhoun had been sworn into office in the Senate Chamber. At the conclusion, cheers again rent the air. The oath was administered by Chief Justice Marshall and the President took the Bible in his hands, reverently kissed it, and laid it down, then bowed again to the people. The surrounding hills reverberated with the artillery salute. The ship's cable broke and there was a rush to reach the President's hand, but he disappeared into the Capitol and left by the west door where he mounted a horse and rode down the avenue.

The morning paper had announced that "the President will proceed to the President's house where he will receive his fellow citizens." They raced after him down the avenue, in carriages and wagons and carts and on foot, wearing hickory nut necklaces, carrying hickory canes and brooms, riding on horses with hickory bark bridles, and shouting "Jackson Forever!" and "Hurra' for Jackson!" At the White House, "it was the People's day, and the People's President and the People would rule." Men with muddy boots stood on damask satin-covered chairs and orange punch drenched the furniture to the accompaniment of breaking china and crystal. A mob of well-wishers backed the President to the wall and he escaped only when a semi-circle of men formed

View of the city of Washington in 1833, from beyond the Navy Yard, painted by G. Cooke, was engraved by W. J. Bennett, published by Lewis P. Clover. The Capitol stands out prominently on the hill, at right, with the White House in the distance, left center.

to protect him. He scrambled out a window to return to Gadsby's. White House servants carted tubs of punch out on the south lawn for the mob of twenty thousand, and pandemonium reigned.

That evening the mourning President was well represented at the inaugural ball at Carusi's Assembly Room by his private secretary who was a nephew of Mrs. Jackson's, Andrew Jackson Donelson, and his lovely wife, Emily. The ball was handsome, the supper elegant, and about 350 ladies and 400 gentlemen attended, though for his five-dollar ticket a gentleman could bring two ladies.

The new President, much fatigued, dined at Gadsby's with Vice President Calhoun and a few friends on a sirloin of a prize ox sent to him by New York butcher John Merkle. Before the close of his inaugural day the President wrote a note to the donor:

"Permit me, sir, to assure you of the gratification which I felt in being enabled to place on my table so fine a specimen of your market, and to offer my sincere thanks for so acceptable a token of your regard for my character."

Andrew Jackson's second inauguration was a quiet affair in the hall of the House of Representatives on Monday, March 4, 1833. Snow lay on the ground and it was a cold, bright day. All plans for a public demonstration were cancelled because the 65-year-old President's health was not good.

The ailing President was assisted into his closed carriage, which hurried along the slushy avenue from the White House to the Capitol. He was met at the east front by the Mayor of the city of Washington and the council members, the first time the city as a corporation figured in the inaugural ceremonies.

At noon the President and his new Vice President-elect, Martin Van Buren, entered the Hall of Representatives. The President took the Speaker's seat with Van Buren on his left and Donelson, his private secretary, on his right. A few minutes later Jackson rose, was greeted by cheers from the large assembly, and proceeded to deliver his address in an audible and firm voice. Cheers and applause followed.

Then the venerable Chief Justice Marshall stepped forward and, for the ninth and last time, administered the oath. He had performed this honorable duty for five Presidents. The oath was also administered to Vice President Van Buren, who did not make an address. Then, amid applause, Jackson and Van Buren departed.

The President's house was opened to visitors from half past two o'clock to half past four o'clock, but "the ceremonies of the Inauguration and the Levee . . . were too much for the shattered constitution of the President," reported one observer. "His attendants were obliged to take him abruptly from the drawing room and carry him to bed."

Two brilliant balls were held that evening, the Inauguration Ball at Carusi's and the Republican Citizen's Inauguration Ball Civil and Military at Central Masonic Hall. The President was represented by both the young Donelsons and by his adopted son, Andrew, Jr., and his petite bride, Sarah. But the old President was home in bed, leafing through Rachel's Bible and gazing fondly at her lovely miniature portrait which he wore on a cord around his neck.

MARTIN VAN BUREN

☆　☆　☆

March 4, 1837

Martin Van Buren, the first President of the United States born under the United States flag, was the protégé of President Jackson, who got up from his sickbed to accompany the 54-year-old President-elect to the inaugural ceremonies on Saturday, March 4, 1837. Two days before Jackson had written to a friend: "On March 4 I hope to be able to go up to the Capitol to witness the glorious scene of Van Buren—once rejected by the Senate—sworn into office by Chief Justice Taney, also once rejected by the same factious Senate."

"Captain Mason's fine volunteer troop of dragoons" and "Captains Blake's and Bronaugh's very handsome companies of volunteer infantry" escorted the retiring and incoming Presidents, who rode in an elegant phaeton constructed of fine-grained, unpainted, highly polished oak from the frigate *Constitution*, drawn by Jackson's four iron-gray carriage horses with handsome brass-mounted harnesses. Its one seat held two persons, with a high box for the driver in front. On each coach door was a painting of "Old Ironsides" in full sail. One observer who watched the two ride by was struck with admiration by the venerable appearance of Jackson and by the peaceful and dignified manner of the President-elect.

As the procession of dignitaries emerged on the inaugural platform at the east portico of the Capitol on the clear, cold day, " a cheer greeted the old hero," reported chronicler Ben Perley Poore, "and a smile of satisfaction lit up his wan, stern features as he stood leaning on his cane with one hand and holding with the other his crape-bound white fur hat, while he acknowledged the compliment paid him by a succession

42

Martin Van Buren, lithograph portrait by Charles Fenderich

View of the Capitol from Pennsylvania Avenue, on the west side, during the 1830's shows the lombardy poplars flourishing.

of bows." Then Van Buren stepped to the front of the platform and read his inaugural address in a clear, distinct voice. Shortly before, he had witnessed Colonel Richard M. Johnson take the oath of office as Vice President in the Senate Chamber.

Van Buren was about five feet six, of Dutch ancestry with a "bright blond" complexion and a "rather exquisite appearance," said a contemporary. The son of a Kinderhook, New York, tavern keeper, he was so dapper and elegant in manners, dress, and refined tastes that his opponents charged he was no Democrat. But his good friend, William Allen Butler, defended his rare individuality. "Where he acquired that peculiar neatness and polish of manner which he wore so lightly, and which served every turn of domestic, social and political intercourse, I do not know," Butler said. "As you saw him once, you saw him always —always punctilious, always polite, always cheerful, always self-possessed. It seemed to anyone who studied this phase of his character as if, in some early moment of his destiny, his whole nature had been bathed in cool, clear and unruffled depth, from which it drew this lifelong serenity and self-control."

At the conclusion of the address, Chief Justice Roger Taney administered the oath, the new President kissed the Bible, and General Jackson shook his hand cordially as national salutes were fired by nearby military stations. The populace cheered and the bands played "Hail to the Chief" as other dignitaries congratulated the President. Then Van

This wood engraving, incorrectly identified as the "Inauguration of M. Van Buren, March 4, 1837," when it appeared in the Weekly Herald *in 1841, actually depicts the inauguration of Van Buren as Vice President, on March 4, 1833, for the second administration of Andrew Jackson, in the Hall of Representatives.*

A party of distinguished Bostonians in Washington for the inauguration of Van Buren spent the night in the shaving chairs of a barber shop. Others slept on bundles of hay in the markethouse, for though money could buy the most delicious meal in town, there weren't enough beds to accommodate all the strangers who poured into the capital.

Buren and Jackson returned to the mansion, followed by a "promiscuous" crowd that swept by, for three hours, to congratulate the new President and say good-bye to his predecessor.

The Diplomatic Corps were received at four o'clock by the President, who astonished the representatives of royal courts by addressing them as the "democratic corps." Someone gave him a mental nudge, suggesting that perhaps he really meant to say diplomatic.

The ball that evening at Carusi's was described as the most magnificent thing of its kind ever to take place in the nation's capital. Beautiful women graced the scene and champagne flowed profusely, and the Baltimore Band played for dancing. The widower President made a grand entrance about nine-thirty, attended by his Cabinet officers, and stood on an elevated platform to receive the respects of the company. The President left "before the noon of night" and soon after the party broke up.

Thronged as the streets and public places were, *The National Intelligencer* reported, "everything wore a marked appearance of calmness, and the absence of excitement." The inauguration day of Martin Van Buren seemed to bear the stamp of his own unique personality.

WILLIAM HENRY HARRISON

☆ ☆ ☆

March 4, 1841

When General William Henry Harrison reached Washington by the morning train of cars on February 9, 1841, he was the first President-elect of the United States to arrive in the capital by train prior to his inauguration. Despite falling snow, a multitude of citizens turned out at the depot to greet the "People's Friend," or "Old Tippecanoe," as Harrison was nicknamed. He called on President Van Buren and then went to Virginia to visit, returning to Washington as the guest of Mayor William Winston Seaton a few days before his inauguration. His wife, Anna Symmes Harrison, with whom he had eloped forty-seven years before, had stayed behind in Ohio, too ill to travel in the winter, but she planned to join her husband in the spring.

On Centre Market Square, the Whigs had erected a log cabin, the symbol of the victorious "Log Cabin and Hard Cider" campaign for the non-controversial national hero, plucked from civilian retirement at sixty-eight. Harrison actually lived in a large home in rural Ohio and did not like cider, but no matter: the Whigs triumphed.

Far from being a backwoods frontiersman, Harrison was Virginia-born and educated, the son of Benjamin Harrison, an aristocratic patriot who had signed the Declaration of Independence. The younger Harrison went west with the army and at twenty-seven was the governor of the Indiana Territory.

By the "Glorious Fourth of March," 1841, eager citizens had traveled from all parts of the Union to witness the imposing spectacle. Newspaper reporters were among those sleeping on cots put up in the dining room at Gadsby's, which had erected a log cabin in its coach yard in

46

William Henry Harrison, painted by Albert Gallatin Holt

which to feed the guests. "About half an hour before the dinner is set upon the table, a crowd collects about the door way, and when the bell rings the onslaught is tremendous," wrote one reporter, in town to cover the inauguration. "Wo to the laggard, who makes his appearance two minutes after that intensely agitating crisis! Vainly does he shout 'soup! soup!' or 'beef! beef!' his supplications pass unheeded. He has been anticipated by his more enterprising neighbors."

At sunrise a 26-gun salute—one gun for each state—was fired from the Mall to herald the day, which threatened snow. Shortly after ten o'clock the official procession and interested citizens marched to the President-elect's quarters, a salute of three guns signaling their approach. General Harrison mounted a white charger and followed the circuitous route to the Capitol, bowing repeatedly to the ladies who leaned from windows, smiling and waving their handkerchiefs. The General wore a plain black frock coat and was surrounded by seven citizen marshals wearing yellow scarves, as well as the Marshal of the District of Columbia and his aides.

A deafening shout went up from the solid mass—estimated at fifty or sixty thousand people—who had been patiently waiting for hours on the Capitol grounds when the hero appeared on the inaugural platform at

Invitation to the Tippecanoe Inauguration Ball features a log cabin, symbol of the victorious Whig campaign that sent "Old Tippecanoe" to the White House.

Lithograph depicting General Harrison delivering his inaugural address on the platform erected over the east steps of the Capitol was a popular item for sale by F. Taylor, Washington bookseller.

the east portico. The President-elect was a thin old gentleman whose martial bearing made him appear taller than his five feet eight. He was bareheaded, without overcoat or gloves, facing the piercing northeast wind. He read his address to the nation in accents loud and clear. The old General was fond of ancient history and had sprinkled classical allusions throughout his speech, which lacked a log cabin flavor and ran to almost nine thousand words. Harrison interrupted his address, before delivering the last paragraph, and turned to Chief Justice Taney, who then administered the oath while holding the Bible. As Harrison repeated the oath in solemn, loud, distinct tones, spontaneously the men in the crowd uncovered their heads. Then the President delivered the closing sentences of his address and the cannon roared, announcing to the nation that it had a new Chief Magistrate.

From The New York Herald, *March 5, 1841*

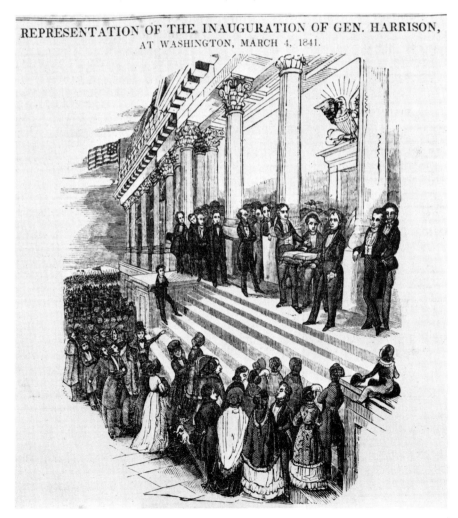

REPRESENTATION OF THE INAUGURATION OF GEN. HARRISON, AT WASHINGTON, MARCH 4, 1841.

Cover illustration for music for quadrilles performed at the Grand Inaugura-
tion Whig Ball held in Boston on March 4, 1841, to celebrate the inaugura-
tion of William Henry Harrison that day in Washington, published and sold
by Henry Prentiss.

Harrison, on horseback, led the procession back to the President's
mansion, cheered as he passed by the immense crowds lining the avenue,
while the bells of the city's churches pealed. And what a colorful procession streamed behind! There were Tippecanoe Clubs, and Georgetown College students in their college uniforms. From the roof of a
log cabin, on a float drawn by horses, fluttered white flags with the
names of states that had voted for "Tippecanoe and Tyler, too"—John
Tyler of Virginia, elected on the Whig slate with Harrison, had already
been sworn into office as Vice President. The most unusual exhibit was
a weaving apparatus, with operators working the machine as it moved
along, drawn by six splendid white horses with bells. As fast as a piece

of cloth was woven, it was plucked from the machine and tossed to the crowd.

The throng followed the President to his new home, but many were left out in the cold because the mansion could hold only a fraction of the well-wishers. The President had issued a mandate about shaking hands, explaining courteously that he was "obliged to decline that mode of saluting his visitors" because his arm had "become painfully affected." The stream of people passed before him, bowing without halting. Then, with the crowd filling all the lower rooms of the house, he slipped away to his chambers upstairs for a brief respite before the inaugural balls.

Gifts for the new President included a richly mounted walking cane made of part of George Washington's coach, and a new coach, a splendid specimen of American craftsmanship, built in Baltimore. Only that morning a Pennsylvania farmer had presented a fatted calf, neatly dressed by his own hands and boxed in ice, which the President received with his thanks "and an expression of his great regard for the agricultural interest of the country."

Former President Van Buren was in the crowd along the route of the inaugural procession which former President John Quincy Adams watched from the window of his F Street home. Adams recorded that the popular celebrations were "unexampled since that of Washington in 1789," but at the same time were conducted "with so much order and tranquillity that not the slightest symptom of conflicting passions occurred to disturb the enjoyment of the day." In the evening fire-balloons and rockets were sent up and there were more artillery salutes.

The President paid a visit to each of the dancing assemblies held in honor of the inauguration and was received with the warmest demonstrations by the crowds. The Inauguration Ball at the New Washington Assembly Rooms on Louisiana Avenue, tickets $10.00, was a magnificent affair that drew some of the most elegant and prominent in the land. Subscription lists for the People's Tippecanoe Inauguration Ball at Carusi's, with tickets at $5.00, had been left at Dr. Watkins's store and at Gadsby's and Brown's Hotels, where all persons desiring to could sign up. As it turned out, it was "got up in superb style" and was more fun. At least the President, the Cabinet officers, and the foreign diplomats apparently thought so, for they went early and stayed late.

JOHN TYLER

☆ ☆ ☆

April 6, 1841

John Tyler was catapulted into the office of the President of the United States just one calendar month after the inauguration of William Henry Harrison, for the old General "died of the presidency in one month," as noted New England sage Ralph Waldo Emerson.

Tyler had returned to his home in Williamsburg, Virginia, after Harrison's inauguration and it was there, at seven o'clock in the morning of Monday, April 5, that Fletcher Webster arrived to deliver an official dispatch notifying Tyler that the President had died the day before. Young Webster, the son of Secretary of State Daniel Webster, had discharged his messenger duties so speedily that one newspaper commented that "the agents of the Post Office might derive some useful hints from him in pushing the mails." Three hours later, Tyler, his two sons, and Webster started for Washington, which they reached at four o'clock Tuesday morning, April 6. Mrs. Tyler—the former Letitia Christian—was an invalid and stayed at home.

Tyler immediately took lodgings at Brown's Indian Queen Hotel and noticed that along Pennsylvania Avenue many shops and warehouses had hung mourning symbols. The tolling of bells and the closing of businesses in Washington and wherever the news had penetrated indicated depth of feeling in all parts of the country.

For the first time in the nation's existence, the person elected to the Vice Presidency had been called upon to assume the powers and duties of the Presidency, under the terms designated by the Constitution. There was no doubt that these duties devolved on Tyler, a former Southern Democrat who had been put on the Whig ticket with Harrison to draw

John Tyler

Southern votes. But there was some confusion as to the rightful successor's title and official procedure, for there was no precedent to go by.

The correspondent of the *Journal of Commerce* reported from Washington on Sunday, April 4, that, "It has been asked whether, under the Constitution, the Vice President is to be the President, and sign his name as President, or as acting President. In reply, I would say, that he becomes THE PRESIDENT in name as well as in substance, and to all intents and purposes just as much so, as if he had been elected President by the people for the same term. But there must be another inauguration.—Mr. Tyler has taken the oath of Vice President, but not the oath of President. He must before he enters upon the duties of the office of President, take the oath prescribed."

The Monday, April 5, *United States Gazette* reported that it had inquiries "as to the future administration of the country." The *Gazette*, after quoting the Constitution, reassured its readers: "It will seem that the death of the President does not render necessary another election; but the Vice President fills his place until the close of the term for which they were both elected."

53

I do solemnly swear that I will faithfully execute the office of President of the United States, and will to the best of my ability, preserve, protect and defend the Constitution of the United States.

John Tyler
, April 6 1841

District of Columbia — City and County of Washington, ss.

I, William Cranch, chief Judge of the Circuit Court of the District of Columbia, certify that, the above named John Tyler personally appeared before me this day, and although he deems himself qualified to perform the duties and exercise the powers and office of President, on the death of William Henry Harrison, late President of the United States, without any other oath than that which he has taken as Vice President; yet as doubts may arise

arise, and for greater caution, took and subscribed the foregoing oath, before me.

W. Cranch.

April 6.th 1841.

The oath of office was signed by John Tyler on April 6, 1841, on Indian Queen Hotel stationery. Certification and comments by Judge W. Cranch, who administered the oath, cast interesting illumination on the first inauguration for a Vice President who succeeded to the office of the Presidency on the death of a President of the United States.

At twelve o'clock on Tuesday, five of the six Cabinet officers called on Tyler at his hotel to pay their respects. He received them with his characteristic politeness and kindness and asked them to stay on in the offices they occupied. After some consultation, the presidential oath of office was formally administered to Tyler by Chief Judge William Cranch of the United States Circuit Court of the District of Columbia, in the presence of the Cabinet.

On a folded letterhead of the Indian Queen Hotel, the constitutional oath was written out, then signed by John Tyler on April 6, 1841, with the endorsement of W. Cranch, who included the interesting footnote to history that Tyler, although he did not think it necessary to take any other oath "than that which he has taken as Vice President; yet as doubts may arise, and for greater caution, took and subscribed the foregoing oath before me."

The decision for Tyler to repeat the constitutional oath was well taken, for doubts did, indeed, arise. Former President Adams was among those who claimed Tyler's title should be "Vice President acting as President."

Newspapers which had referred to Tyler as Vice President in the scheduled funeral arrangements quickly announced that Tyler was President of the United States "and should be so designated by all who have communication with him . . . he will be attended by the heads of the Executive Departments as HIS Cabinet."

The new President, whose manners were those of the old-school Virginia gentleman, promptly paid a visit of mourning at the White House, and General Harrison's relatives "were deeply affected by the delicate terms in which Mr. Tyler tendered to them the occupancy of the House." John Tyler was then fifty-one years old, six feet tall and slender, with thin auburn hair, bluish-gray eyes, and a prominent nose.

"The expression of his face was mild and pleasant, and his manner was remarkably unaffected, gentlemanly, and agreeable. I thought that in his whole carriage and demeanour, he became his station singularly well," Charles Dickens wrote of the new President after visiting the White House.

Brown's Indian Queen Hotel, a few doors east of the Centre Market on Pennsylvania Avenue, was the site of Tyler's inaugural-oath-taking ceremony as well as the scene of several inaugural balls in early nineteenth-century Washington.

Tyler was dubbed "His Accidency" by some, and former President Adams declared in his diary that a strict constructionist of the Constitution would have "more than a doubt whether the Vice President has the right to occupy the President's house or to claim his salary without an act of Congress," noting, "He moved into the house two days ago." There the venerable former President, now a member of the United States House of Representatives, called on Tyler, who apologized to the elder statesman for not having visited him.

Tyler stood firm in his decision to be President of the United States, with all its powers and privileges as well as duties, in his own name. He issued an inaugural address to the people of the United States, which was printed in newspapers throughout the land. The ship of state and shocked citizens had survived the sudden trauma of the death of the President, and the transition of power to the person elected Vice President, for the first time. To John Tyler the nation is indebted for establishing the precedent that the Vice President, on assuming the responsibilities of the highest office in the land, becomes the President of the United States.

JAMES K. POLK

☆ ☆ ☆

March 4, 1845

James K. Polk delivered his inaugural address to "a large assemblage of umbrellas," noted former President Adams, on March 4, 1845. The spectators, who had come from far and near, were drenched. The foreign ministers arrived early to take their places for the ceremonies only to find that the Capitol grounds were closed to carriages because no one on the committee for arrangements had anticipated rain. The courtly ministers in their magnificent uniforms were forced to alight at a side gate and slosh through the mud and downpour to the Senate entrance, their plumed headdresses and gold-braid epaulettes wilting as they walked.

The President-elect and his predecessor, President Tyler, braved the elements to ride in an open carriage, flanked by the Fairfax Cavalry, and Pennsylvania Avenue was so slippery with mud that soldiers fell ingloriously in the procession. Firing at dawn had announced the important day, and between eleven and twelve o'clock President-elect Polk left Coleman's National Hotel to join President Tyler in his carriage, which was escorted by the Marshal of the District of Columbia, General Alexander Hunter, and his assistants. The military led the way to the Capitol, and the Independent Blues of Baltimore, excellently disciplined, made a spendid showing with "Deem's strong and skillful band of musicians." As President and Mrs. Tyler arrived at the hotel, the red-jacketed Empire Club cheered, fired a mounted brass cannon several times, then followed in the procession and fired the cannon later at the Capitol.

The procession entered the Capitol grounds about noon in the cold,

Left: *The "assemblage of umbrellas" at the Capitol for the inauguration of James Knox Polk is the most prominent feature of this wood engraving from the* Illustrated London News. Right: *Full length sketch of Polk shows dashing long cape he wore on his inaugural day.*

The inaugural procession of Polk from the Capitol to the White House following his inauguration was delineated for New York Herald *readers in the March 6, 1845, issue.*

Portrait of James Knox Polk, painted by G. P. A. Healy at the White House in 1846, now hangs in his ancestral home in Columbia, Tennessee.

steady, unrelenting rain. The downpour failed to deter the crowds that had assembled hours before to see the new President, who soon emerged on the platform over the steps at the east portico. The new Vice President, George M. Dallas, had taken the oath in the Senate Chamber.

James Polk stepped forward to read his inaugural address, which few heard. Despite the dreary day, there were a few bright spots in the background. The foremost American portrait painter and inventor, Samuel F.B. Morse, sat on the inaugural platform tapping out, in the code that bears his name, the events of the day on the electric telegraph he had invented just the year before. These telegraphic messages were transmitted to Baltimore, setting a record in reporting the inaugural ceremonies to another city.

Sarah Childress Polk, a handsome, dark-haired and dark-eyed woman, was seated on the inaugural platform, too, proudly sharing her husband's triumph as she had shared his political ambitions and career during the years when he had served as Speaker of the United States House of Representatives and as Governor of Tennessee. She wore a long velvet cloak of rich purplish-blue, fashioned with a deeply fringed cape, and her velvet bonnet was trimmed with satin ribbon.

Polk, who had been picked as a winner by old Andrew Jackson, was so spare that his coat was generally two or three sizes too large. He had dark, penetrating gray eyes, a full, angular brow, and firm mouth, and he wore his silver-touched hair long and brushed back behind his ears. When he concluded reading his address, Chief Justice Taney administered the oath. As the 49-year-old President kissed the Bible, the customary artillery salutes boomed forth. The President was then escorted back to the President's house by an indirect route to avoid slippery Pennsylvania Avenue. There was a reception in the afternoon, but sky-rockets were cancelled because of the weather.

Former President Tyler and his lovely young second wife, Julia, had entertained at an elegant dinner party for their successors only the night before. They received a stream of callers in their hotel suite on the inauguration afternoon, then tried to take "French leave" of Washington the morning after the inauguration. But they missed the boat and spent another day receiving a throng of visitors.

There were two inaugural balls, one at Carusi's at $10.00 a ticket, for

First Lady Sarah Childress Polk chose this gown of blue ribbed silk and satin, trimmed with blonde lace and figured blue ribbon, for the inaugural balls. With the beautiful gown, made by Worth of Paris, she carried an ivory-handled inaugural fan—given to her by her husband especially for the occasion—with portraits of all the Presidents of the United States painted on one side and on the other an oval painting depicting the signing of the Declaration of Independence.

Scrambling for supper at the two-dollar inaugural ball for "pure Democrats" at the National Theatre, 1845.

all political parties, and the other for "pure Democrats" at $2.00 a ticket at the National Theatre. Party rivalries had not only led to the two balls but also to a roaring mix-up in the guest lists. When the inaugural committee unwittingly failed to invite the Diplomatic Corps to the official ball, the slighted representatives of royal courts accepted invitations to the two-dollar jamboree, where a foreign minister's lady was seen dancing in the same quadrille with her gardener.

The President and Mrs. Polk attended both balls, and at their entrance to each the band struck up "Hail to the Chief." Mrs. Polk was stunning in a Parisian gown of blue silk and satin, but she didn't dance. Sarah Polk, for all her warmth and charm, was a strict Calvinist and disapproved of such frivolity. For the first time in the history of inaugural balls, the ten-dollar ball showed a profit and the surplus, over $1000, was divided between two orphan asylums. But the President and his lady "supped with the true blue 2 dollar democracy," reported old former President Adams, who had declined an invitation to take part in the inaugural ceremonies.

ZACHARY TAYLOR

☆ ☆ ☆

March 5, 1849

General Zachary Taylor was sixty-four and had never exercised his right to vote in a presidential election before the one in 1848 which sent him to the White House. The old career soldier, who had earned a commission as a major general and the nickname of "Old Rough and Ready" from his troops, had been the compromise candidate of the Whig party. He had first gained recognition as an Indian fighter in the Florida swamps, but he became a national hero as the victor of Palo Alto and Buena Vista in the Mexican War. Since March 4, 1849, fell on Sunday, the inauguration was postponed until Monday, and no one seemed concerned that the country was without a President for a day.

The old soldier, whose plain-spoken frankness and goodwill were as well known among his troops as were his stubbornness and courage, came from Virginia gentry stock. A second cousin, James Madison, had been the fourth President of the United States. In February, when the President-elect set out from his Baton Rouge, Louisiana, home for the long journey north to Washington, he left behind his wife and inseparable companion, Margaret, who had shared tents and cabins to make a home for her husband. Old Zach used to claim that his wife "had made a nightly prayer . . . that Henry Clay might be elected President in his place." But it was illness, not stubbornness, that kept her from being at her husband's side during the triumphal journey to the capital. In her place to act as the President-elect's official hostess was their attractive 24-year-old daughter, Betty, accompanied by her husband of less than a year, Major William W. Bliss, who had been adjutant to General Taylor.

Zachary Taylor

It was long after dark when the President-elect's train arrived at the railway station at the corner of Pennsylvania Avenue and Third Street. Bonfires had been lit along the train route from the Relay House in Maryland, where the party had changed to the train for Washington. Greeted with more bonfires and a flight of rockets, combined with the booming of cannon, Taylor stepped off and exclaimed, "Oh, for a bed!"

"Hooray for Old Zach!" responded the crowd that followed his carriage down the avenue, now lighted with solar gaslights, to Willard's Hotel. There, several days later, he met members of the inaugural committee. Senator Jefferson Davis of Mississippi unfurled and read a parchment scroll, and the moment was an especially poignant one to the gray-haired old man, who "listened with downcast eyes." Taylor's oldest daughter, Sarah, had eloped with Davis, then a young West Point graduate, some years before and had died shortly after her marriage. Taylor had disapproved of the elopement and it was not until the Battle of Buena Vista that the old General and his former son-in-law were recon-

This street scene, showing the new gaslight lampposts installed along Pennsylvania Avenue during the Polk administration, pictures the White House as it looked when Taylor became President. The columned north portico was added during Jackson's first administration.

ciled. For the rest of their lives, both Davis and his second wife were considered members of the Taylor family.

The President-elect called on President Polk and was, in turn, entertained on March 1 at a large dinner party served in the White House French cook's best style. On Saturday, March 3, President and Mrs. Polk moved from the mansion to the Irving Hotel, and here military bands serenaded them on Sunday evening. Mrs. Polk, who had once stopped the music on board a riverboat on a Sunday, was not to be seen but the President appeared at the window, and eventually collapsed of exhaustion after the troubadours left.

Long before breakfast hour on the inaugural day, the bells rang out and martial music resounded along the city's avenues, while throngs of people were wending their way to the Capitol. It was cloudy, the air flecked with snow. At nine o'clock, the hundred gentlemen designated as marshals for the inauguration rode in a body to Willard's Hotel to pay their respects to the President-elect. There they lined up in the hall and General Taylor, on the arm of Mayor Seaton, shook hands with the men. At half-past eleven, the inaugural procession fell into line directly behind the chief marshal and his aides.

The President-elect, in a plain black suit, rode in a carriage drawn by four handsome gray horses and surrounded by the hundred citizen marshals. The place of honor immediately in front was reserved for the few—the very few and very old—veterans of the Revolutionary War and the War of 1812, as well as the officers and soldiers who had served with General Taylor in the Florida and Mexican campaigns. The procession halted at the Irving Hotel and President Polk was escorted to the carriage, where he was seated at the right of General Taylor, who shook hands cordially. Hundreds of star-spangled banners of every size and fabric waved in the breeze along the avenue.

President Polk practically fell out of the carriage from surprise when the President-elect expressed his opinion that "California and Arizona were too distant to become members of the Union and that it would be better for them to be an independent government." The outgoing President, who had presided over the acquisition of those territories following the Mexican War, later declared in his diary, "These are alarming opinions to be entertained by the President of the U.S." But at the moment he and the inaugural escort were speechless, while General Taylor took off his hat, from time to time, and waved to the people.

At the east front of the Capitol, General Taylor and President Polk walked out together and were seated on a sofa at the edge of the inaugu-

This engraving depicting the inauguration of General Taylor, after a drawing by Wm. Croome, engraved by Brightly & Keyser, was dedicated to the various Rough and Ready Clubs throughout the Union.

ral platform. The President-elect read his address in a low voice, and it was obvious that he was a popular favorite with the assembled thousands, who cheered vociferously. Then Chief Justice Taney administered the oath of office. Former President Polk immediately stepped forward and shook the new President's hand, saying to him: "I hope, Sir, the country may be prosperous under your administration." Amid the firing of cannon and the music of bands, the President and former President re-entered their carriage and were escorted back down the broad avenue. Again the procession halted for James Polk, who took leave of the President at the Irving Hotel. There he and Mrs. Polk greeted friends until time to board the steamboat, at three o'clock in the morning, to travel by the southern route to their Tennessee home.

At the White House President Taylor gallantly received the salutes of thousands, "taking the Ladies each by the hand—a ceremony which for their great number it was not possible for him to go through with the multitude of the other sex."

President Taylor and Vice President Millard Fillmore, who had been sworn into office that day in the Senate Chamber, attended each of the three inaugural balls, beginning with one for the visiting military at Carusi's. Then they went on to Jackson Hall, between Third and Four-and-a-Half Streets on Pennsylvania Avenue, where the Germania Band of Philadelphia played, and there the honored guests had refreshments from the elegantly spread supper table. The President's daughter wore a dainty white silk ball gown and charmed all with her girlish freshness and enthusiasm.

The President and Vice President and their escorts then re-entered their carriages and proceeded to the Grand Inauguration Ball in a great frame pavillion, especially erected for the occasion, adjoining the City Hall on Judiciary Square. The crowd of four thousand was standing to receive the new Chief Magistrate. As he appeared at the head of and descended the broad flight of steps which led down to the dancing saloon, loud acclamations and cheers rent the air. The din was so deafening that even the music of Gung'l's powerful band was drowned out. Boston's Mr. Quincy proposed three cheers for Vice President Fillmore, which were given heartily. The President made his way around the packed saloon, taking "almost every lady by the hand" and receiving the respects of almost every gentleman. Then the guests of honor had refreshments. The President and his party left about half-past midnight, but the celebration continued for hours.

Invitation to the Grand Inauguration Ball features a picture of General Taylor and "Old Whitey," with the Spanish names of the sites of Taylor's victories during the Mexican War.

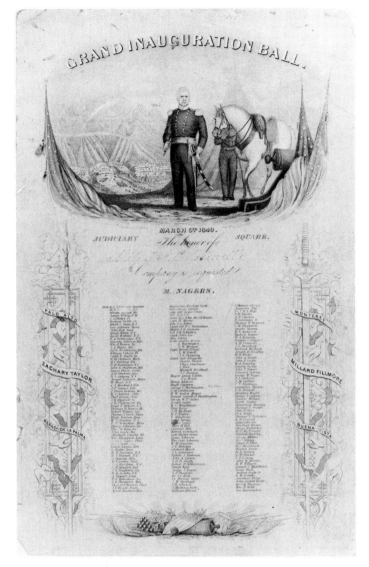

The servants departed long before the dancers did, leaving the wraps in a mess. Among the ballgoers who couldn't find his hat was a one-term Congressman from Illinois who had campaigned for Old Zach. Giving up the search after an hour, the tall, slim man started off across Judiciary Square bareheaded, adjusting his short cloak as he walked, on the long hike to Mrs. Sprigg's boardinghouse on Capitol Hill at four o'clock in the morning. His name was Abraham Lincoln.

MILLARD FILLMORE

☆ ☆ ☆

July 10, 1850

Late on the night of July 9, 1850, Vice President Millard Fillmore answered a knock on the door of his Washington residence. The caller was a messenger from the Department of State bearing a letter which by its salutation conveyed the news that Fillmore dreaded. The short message, signed by the seven Cabinet officers, was addressed to "Millard Fillmore, President of the U. States." The tolling of the State Department bell had begun, echoing the grim intelligence of the letter—that President Taylor had died—and soon the funeral knell was sounding from every church steeple in Washington.

Fillmore sat down and penned a reply to the Cabinet which briefly expressed his shock and grief, and he added: "I shall avail myself of the earliest moment to communicate the sad intelligence to Congress; and shall appoint a time and place for taking the oath of office prescribed to the President of the United States. You are requested to be present and witness the ceremony." Fillmore handed the letter to the messenger, closed the door, and spent a sleepless night alone in the house, for Mrs. Fillmore and their daughter, Mary, were not in Washington.

At sunrise the next morning the national colors, shrouded in black, were flown at half-mast, and sable appeared on all public offices, hotels, and many private dwellings. The White House was literally covered with black, and even the carriage houses of the Cabinet and the horses attached to the Secretaries' carriages were adorned with black.

Early in the day, Fillmore sent a message to his "fellow citizens of the Senate and House of Representatives," announcing President Taylor's death, and proposing to take the oath of office "this day, at 12 o'clock,

68

Millard Fillmore

in the hall of the House of Representatives, in the presence of both Houses of Congress." Crowds of citizens hastened to the Capitol not only to witness the inauguration ceremony but also to listen to the eloquent tributes to the late President. Meanwhile a stream of people kept pouring into the grounds of the executive mansion to pay their last respects to Zachary Taylor.

At twelve o'clock, the Speaker and Members of the House were standing as the Senate entered the hall. Then came the Honorable Millard Fillmore, attended by a member of each House, who took a seat at the Clerk's table.

The new president was fifty years old and a handsome man with white hair, shrewd gray eyes, and a winning, dignified manner. At the age of fifteen he had been apprenticed by his poor parents to a wool carder. Eventually he went to a one-room school nearby where his teacher was a pretty redhead named Abigail Powers. Eight years later they were mar-

The earliest known photograph of the Capitol, from the east garden, was taken by the patent Talbotypeprocess by W & F Langenheim in July, 1850, the month in which Fillmore succeeded to the Presidency.

ried. Fillmore pursued his studies, became a lawyer, and entered politics in New York State.

In the quiet, unostentatious manner for which he became known, Fillmore rose in the Hall of Representatives on July 10, 1850, and "in a clear and distinct voice, pronounced the oath of fidelity to the Constitution, and the act of installation was complete." For the second time, old Judge Cranch had been called upon to administer the oath in an emergency ceremony for a new President. "The profound silence of so great an assemblage of deeply concerned spectators, the ceremony, so brief and so simple, yet so important in its consequences, national, political, and personal, presented an incident and a scene altogether American," reported *The National Intelligencer*.

President Fillmore withdrew from the Capitol quickly and quietly, leaving behind him a message addressed to his "Fellow Citizens of the Senate and the House of Representatives" which was read when the two Houses reconvened separately following the ceremony.

"The sceptre of the People passes into his hands as quietly and as quickly as a power of attorney could be acknowledged before a justice of the peace," commented *The National Intelligencer*, which also noted sagely that though the simple ceremony made less impression on American spectators than other dramatic incidents of the day did, it was the one most impressive to foreigners.

FRANKLIN PIERCE

☆ ☆ ☆

March 4, 1853

Franklin Pierce of New Hampshire, the fourteenth President of the United States, was the first and only one to affirm, rather than swear, to the oath of office at his inauguration on March 4, 1853. The handsome, 48-year-old Pierce, a brigadier general in the Mexican War, had served as both a Representative and later as United States Senator from New Hampshire. After his election to the Presidency, his wife, Jane Appleton Pierce, who hated the life of a politician's wife, sighed and prepared to return to Washington from New Hampshire. But Pierce came to Washington for his inauguration without his wife. Between the election and the inauguration, tragedy struck the family. The Pierces were in a train wreck and saw their only surviving child, 11-year-old Bennie, killed before their eyes as the coach left the rails and plunged down a rocky chasm. The shock was so overwhelming that Mrs. Pierce never fully recovered from it.

The heartsick President-elect arrived in Washington in February accompanied only by his private secretary, Sidney Webster, and a private bodyguard, Thomas O'Neill, his former orderly. He left Mrs. Pierce with friends in Baltimore. There must have been seventy to eighty thousand people within the city limits of Washington—about twice its normal population—for the inauguration, for the Union now consisted of thirty-one states stretching from the Great Lakes to the Gulf and from sea to sea.

Not only did President and Mrs. Fillmore entertain the lonely, saddened President-elect at dinner, but Fillmore took Pierce with him to hear the English author, William Makepeace Thackeray, deliver a lec-

71

Franklin Pierce

ture on English humorists, and also invited Pierce to accompany him on a trip down the Potomac to inspect a new ship. Washington Irving, who was along on the steamer and also attended the inauguration, later wrote to a friend in Europe: "It was admirable to see the quiet and courtesy with which this great transition of power and rule from one party to another took place. I was at festive meetings where the members of the opposite parties mingled socially together, and have seen the two Presidents arm-in-arm as if the sway of an immense empire was not passing from one to another."

On the morning of March 4 a raw, chilling wind was accompanied by occasional snow flurries and the people seemed invigorated as they scurried to the Capitol and gathered along the gaily decorated avenue. President Fillmore called for the President-elect at Willard's Hotel in a magnificent barouche, a gift just two days before from some citizens in Massachusetts to Pierce. The President-elect rode standing upright most of the way to the Capitol, bowing and acknowledging the salutes of the crowds. There was a grand military array in the procession, but perhaps the most popular contingent was the Manhattan Fire Company of New York, No. 8, drawing a splendid, large fire engine, and accompanied by the "unsurpassed 'Dodsworth's Band,'" as reported *The Evening Star*.

The President's party entered the north side gate to the Capitol yard and then walked through a covered way to the north door. Before their arrival, the new Senators had been sworn in and Senator David Atchison of Missouri had been re-chosen to serve as President pro tempore of the Senate. The new Vice President, William R. King, was in Cuba and on that very day took the oath of office administered by United States Consul Thomas Rodney.

Snow fell in rapid flakes and the raw March winds sent shivers through the twenty thousand spectators as Pierce stepped forward on the inaugural platform and, holding up his right hand, affirmed the oath administered by Chief Justice Taney. Mrs. Fillmore, who had established the first library in the White House (there was nary a book in the place, not even a Bible, when she moved in), stood on the platform between two literary giants—England's Thackeray and America's Irving. But the bitter weather proved fatal to Abigail Fillmore. She caught cold, and died less than a month later.

The new President delivered his inaugural address from memory in a clear, strong voice and with a winning manner that indicated great nervous energy. At the conclusion, as the artillery thundered, the President

This woodcut, showing Pierce leaving Willard's Hotel, appeared in the Illustrated London News.

The inauguration of Pierce was captured in this contemporary wood engraving.

withdrew into the warm Senate for a few moments. Escorted by the military, the presidential carriage returned to the President's mansion where former President Fillmore took leave of the new President and returned to Willard's. There his arrival at the front door was hailed by hearty cheers.

At the White House, President Pierce received the congratulations of the people who quickly crossed the oval drawing room, now known as the Blue Room, and left by the south portico of the mansion. There was no further celebration because the President was mourning his son.

It was dark by the time President Pierce and Sidney Webster were left alone in the big mansion. In vain they rang for servants, but there was no reply, and no one to show them to the living quarters on the floor above. With a candle in hand, President Pierce and his secretary climbed the stairs to the second floor, searched the rooms left in disarray by the departing Fillmores, and, after an exhausting day, settled down for their first night's sleep in the White House.

JAMES BUCHANAN

☆ ☆ ☆

March 4, 1857

Bachelor James Buchanan had a distinguished, stately air about him as he rode down Pennsylvania Avenue to his inauguration on March 4, 1857, and, indeed, the six feet tall, white-haired man had served his country as an ambassador abroad. As the spectators tossed flowers into the open carriage carrying the two handsome Presidents to the Capitol, cheers drowned out the band music. The procession, like the inaugural ball to come, was a brilliant success, befitting a man who proceeded to preside over the White House as though it were a republican court.

The elaborate barouche bearing the President-elect and President Pierce had joined the procession—to the accompaniment of cheers—when it arrived at the National Hotel about twelve o'clock. People from every state and territory of the Union—even New Mexico, Utah, Washington, and Oregon territories—were among the crowd of 150,000 in the capital to watch the inaugural festivities. The colorful procession on the bright, beautiful day was headed by a battalion of Marines, with the Marine Band in showy scarlet uniforms, and the marshals with yellow, blue, or pink scarves and gaily coordinated saddle covers for their horses. The Keystone Club of Philadelphia acted as personal bodyguard for Pennsylvania's native son, the 65-year-old President-elect, and surrounded his carriage.

The carriage immediately behind the Presidents' carried James Buchanan Henry, nephew and private secretary to the President-elect, and naval surgeon Dr. Jonathon Foltz, who was never far from Buchanan's side on inauguration day and quietly administered remedies to his presidential patient from time to time. Buchanan was suffering from a gastro-

Woodcut portrait of "Our New President," James Buchanan, appeared in Harper's Weekly.

intestinal infection which had struck a number of guests at the National Hotel. One of those stricken in the epidemic was Buchanan's nephew, Colonel E. E. Lane, who died just three weeks after the inauguration.

Two symbolic floats followed in the inaugural procession. One was a full-rigged ship, a miniature of the historic frigate *Constitution;* the second was a Liberty float, with a woman representing the Goddess of Liberty seated by a flagpole fifty feet high. The military in the procession reached the north gate of the Capitol, opened ranks facing inward, and formed a double line of soldiers through which rolled the barouche carrying the two Presidents.

President Pierce followed President-elect Buchanan onto the outdoor platform at the east portico after Vice President John C. Breckenridge took the oath in the Senate Chamber. Buchanan was greeted with resounding shouts and cheers and, in turn, bowed repeatedly, with his hat in his hand. He was dressed in his famous black Lancaster suit, made and presented to him by the Pennsylvania city near his Wheatland estate. The black satin lining of the coat was stitched with symbols of the thirty-one states centered by the Keystone, the symbol of Pennsylvania. The President-elect read his address in a clear, distinct tone to the fifty thousand spectators, then turned and, with his hand on his small, elegant peach-velvet-covered Bible, took the oath administered by Chief Justice Taney.

As former President Pierce and others stepped forward to congratulate the new President there was a 31-gun salute—one gun for each state. The two Presidents were escorted back to the White House and the doors were opened to the crowd. The Pierces were houseguests for several days before they returned to New Hampshire. During the afternoon Mr. Elliot, the aeronaut, made a balloon ascension. After hovering over eastern Washington in a stationary position the balloon floated off over Bladensburg, Maryland, to the fascinated delight of all who saw it.

On the night of the inauguration, the President attended the magnificent Grand National Inauguration Ball, held in an enormous temporary building on Judiciary Square. Attired in his Lancaster suit, he

Spectacular float in the Buchanan inaugural procession was this miniature of the U.S.S. Constitution, *made by mechanics at the Navy Yard. Sailors climbed about in the rigging during the parade while the float was drawn by horses along Pennsylvania Avenue.*

arrived about eleven o'clock with his lovely 26-year-old niece, Harriet Lane, who had been hostess of the American Embassy in London for her bachelor uncle and was now to act as First Lady of the White House during his administration. She swept regally into the inaugural ball, wearing a white dress with many strands of seed pearls around her throat.

The table in the supper room was crowned by a pyramid of cake four feet high decorated with a flag bearing the arms of each State and Territory. Three thousand dollars was spent for the wine alone and the feast included 400 gallons of oysters, 500 quarts of chicken salad, 500 quarts of jellies, 1200 quarts of ice cream, eight rounds of beef, 75 hams, 60 saddles of mutton and four of venison, 125 tongues, and patés of every description.

The President with his niece and Vice President Breckenridge wined

This is the first known photographic record of an inauguration, taken at Buchanan's, March 4, 1857. The ceremony took place on the open platform, with guard rail, erected over the steps at the east portico of the Capitol. Note that the new Senate wing of the Capitol, right, was still not completed.

The Buchanan Grand National Inauguration Ball, held in an immense temporary building erected on Judiciary Square, was a magnificent affair. The walls were lined with red, white and blue draperies and decorated with the flags of all nations. The ceiling of white cloth, studded with golden stars, glittered and reflected the warm glow from the enormous gaslight chandeliers.

and dined and enjoyed the ball for two hours. They left about a half-hour after midnight but the dancing continued until dawn. The inauguration ball—the most magnificent ever—was a splendid memory that had to last the Democrats a long, long time—twenty-eight years.

ABRAHAM LINCOLN

☆ ☆ ☆

March 4, 1861   March 4, 1865

Never before had the inauguration of a President taken place under such perilous conditions. The nation was trembling on the brink of war when Abraham Lincoln of Illinois, who had been elected by only 40 per cent of the popular vote, was inaugurated on March 4, 1861. Seven Southern states had already seceded from the Union, and just two weeks earlier Jefferson Davis had been inaugurated as President of the Confederate States of America in Montgomery, Alabama. The Confederate flag was flying in Alexandria, George Washington's hometown just across the Potomac River from Washington, and there were fears that an assassination attempt would be made on Lincoln's life.

The 52-year-old Republican President-elect had slipped into Washington by an unannounced route because of a suspected plot against his train. General-in-Chief of the United States Army Winfield Scott, then seventy years old, insisted, over President Buchanan's objections, on unprecedented security precautions for inauguration day, so convinced was he that Lincoln's life was in danger. The city of Washington bristled with bayonets, and the Washington Rifles, in full uniform, were stationed in squads on rooftops along Pennsylvania Avenue. One gay crowd that had come to the capital for the great day was surprised to turn down a side streeet and find mounted cannon, with artillery men standing ready to fire, on both sides of the street.

Lincoln himself had warned a friend: "Don't let your wife come to my inauguration. It is best for our women to remain indoors on that day as the bullets may be flying." But with the calm that a contemporary described as "impassive as an Indian martyr," Lincoln rode in an open

Abraham Lincoln, with a new, full beard, arrived in Washington on February 23, 1861, and a short time later—probably the following day—sat for photographs in Brady's Photographic Parlor.

Mary Todd Lincoln was photographed in several elegant new gowns, a few days before her husband's inauguration in 1861, by Brady or one of his assistants.

barouche along Pennsylvania Avenue with President Buchanan, who had called for Lincoln at Willard's. The two men took their seats in the barouche, with the military at "present arms" and the band playing "Hail to the Chief," and the carriage moved on, flanked by a mounted guard so dense that it was practically impossible to get a glimpse of the President-elect, which may have been exactly what General Scott intended. Soldiers lined the streets and a company of Sappers and Miners preceded the presidential carriage.

Tornadoes of dust swirled along as the procession moved down the avenue. The skies had brightened, a good sign, by the time the Presidents arrived at the Capitol. The morning had dawned with leaden skies. While the Presidential party was in the Capitol, a little man with bushy red whiskers perched in a tall tree in front of the east portico and delivered a lecture on the vices of the times. He descended, after bestowing a fatherly benediction on all, and was marched off to the guardhouse.

A shout of welcome greeted Lincoln's appearance on the inaugural platform, where a crude wooden canopy had been constructed, and

Lincoln, accompanied by President Buchanan, waves his hat from the presidential carriage as it rolls along Pennsylvania Avenue to the Capitol for the inauguration, March 4, 1861. The scene was sketched for Frank Leslie's Illustrated Newspaper.

Photograph of Lincoln's first inauguration shows crude wooden canopy erected on the inaugural platform to protect the presidential party from rain.

the unfinished new Capitol dome, surrounded by scaffolding, loomed above. The Marine Band struck up national airs and played, most delightfully, for a few minutes. Then Senator E. D. Baker of Oregon rose and presented the new President, who had grown a beard since the election, adding a softer, dignified note to his awkward appearance. He wore a plain black broadcloth suit.

When the gangling, six feet four President-elect rose to address the audience, he put his new gold-headed cane under the table, but he fumbled awkwardly with his silk top hat. Quickly Senator Stephen Douglas of Illinois, a competitor for the Presidency, leaned forward and took the shining new hat so that the President could get on with his inaugural address. Lincoln unfurled the galley proof on which his speech was printed, put on steel-bowed spectacles, and read his speech. Among the thirty thousand spectators were four men who were destined to become President—Rutherford B. Hayes and James Garfield of Ohio, Chester Arthur of New York, and Benjamin Harrison of Indiana.

At the conclusion of the 35-minute address, 84-year-old Chief Justice Taney arose. He had, said one lady, "the face of a galvanized corpse," and this was the seventh and last time that he administered the oath to a President. Lincoln repeated the oath with his hand lying on the open Bible.

General Scott was in the background, carefully observing the entire

NEW YORK
ILLUSTRATED NEWS

No. 71.—Vol. III.   NEW-YORK, SATURDAY, MARCH 16, 1861.   Price Six Cents.

OPEN THIS PAPER WITH CARE BEFORE YOU CUT IT.

Chief Justice Roger Taney, right, administers the oath of office to Lincoln at the east front of the Capitol, March 4, 1861, with James Buchanan at left. From a sketch by Thomas Nast.

MR. LINCOLN TAKING THE OATH OF OFFICE IN THE FRONT OF THE CAPITOL. From a Sketch by Thos. Nast   see page 304.

scene, with a battery of flying artillery stationed on the brow of the hill not far from the north entrance to the Capitol. Fortunately, the artillery was needed only to thunder its salute while President Lincoln and "plain Mr. Buchanan" were escorted by the military to the White House. Arriving there, President Lincoln was met by General Scott, who had hurried on ahead to have the mansion in readiness for its rightful owner. On the threshold, former President Buchanan warmly shook his successor's hand, conveying his heartfelt best wishes for Lincoln's personal happiness and the nation's peace and prosperity.

The most appealing float in the procession was draped in red, white, and blue to symbolize the Constitution and the Union, with little girls, each dressed in white with a laurel wreath on her head, representing

The crowd clustered in front of the east portico of the Capitol for Lincoln's inauguration in 1861. Note scaffolding on roof for the unfinished new dome.

the States and Territories and Liberty. At the White House the youngsters called on President Lincoln, who promptly picked up each little girl and kissed her. Then the doors of the mansion were opened to the thousands who waited to shake hands with the President. He was "in excellent spirits, and gave each of his friends a cordial grasp and a smile," reported *The National Intelligencer.*

That evening a splendid ball brought the day to a close. Soldiers surrounded the hall, shaped like a parallelogram and decorated with red and white muslin, erected on Judiciary Square. Shortly after eleven, when the dancing had started, the band struck up "Hail Columbia" and President Lincoln entered on the arms of Vice President Hannibal Hamlin and Senator Henry Anthony of Rhode Island. To the astonishment of all, Mrs. Lincoln followed on the arm of Senator Douglas, the President's old political rival popularly known as the "Little Giant." Mary Todd Lincoln wore a gown of rich watered silk with an elegant point lace cape and pearl jewelry with camelias in her hair.

The ballroom was full of beautifully costumed women whose bright eyes and jewels flashed merrily as they danced with the distinguished guests. Commented one reporter, "no one would have imagined that a cloud was in our national heaven." Only President Lincoln looked weary and worn.

Four years later, on the morning of Saturday, March 4, 1865, when the military arrived at the White House to escort Lincoln to his second inauguration, the President was already at the Capitol working. The marshals and military then surrounded the carriage carrying Mrs. Lincoln and the Senate committee, and the cheering crowd, standing in a sea of mud along the avenue, thought the closed carriage contained the President.

Following days of capricious weather and rain, the morning was miserable, with wind "like whirling demons" that uprooted trees, and dark, "with slanting rain, full of rage," as noted poet Walt Whitman, who lived in Washington. "Black plaster" was thick in the streets. The Army Corps of Engineers had even taken soundings on the avenue with the plan of laying pontoons from the Capitol to the White House, but abandoned the idea when it found that the bottom was too soft to hold anchors. *The Evening Star* reported that police were confining to the sidewalks all pedestrians who could not swim, although some dashed recklessly into the avenue at shallow crossings.

While ball guests danced in the temporary hall, shaped like a parallelogram and decorated with red and white muslin, in honor of Lincoln's inauguration in 1861, soldiers surrounded the structure erected especially for the occasion on Judiciary Square.

Around the Capitol, over 30,000 people waited patiently in the deep mud for Lincoln's second inauguration at the east front of the Capitol, March 4, 1865. Gleaming new Capitol dome towers above the impressive scene, which ap-peared in Frank Leslie's Illustrated Newspaper.

Lincoln, standing by the small round table, center, reads the most memorable inaugural address in the nation's history at his second inauguration, March 4, 1865. Photograph by Matthew Brady or an assistant.

Around the Capitol, over thirty thousand people waited patiently in the deep mud. "As the President came out on the capitol portico, a curious little white cloud, the only one in that part of the sky, appear'd like a hovering bird right over him," Whitman recorded. When the President, in his unassuming way, stepped out from the columns in view of the throng, loud, long cheers rose repeatedly to meet him. Chief Justice Salmon Chase administered the oath. The President, dressed as usual in a black suit, repeated it with his hand on a red, plush-covered Bible. Then in a clear voice he read his second inaugural address, a declaration of peace goals for the war-weary nation. It concluded with the compassionate words long since carved in the Lincoln Memorial and in the hearts of his countrymen:

"With malice toward none; with charity for all; with firmness in the right, as God gives us to see the right, let us strive on to finish the work we are in; to bind up the nation's wounds; to care for him who shall have borne the battle, and for his widow and his orphan; to do all which may achieve and cherish a just and a lasting peace, among ourselves, and with all nations."

As he concluded, a battery of Naval howitzers fired a salute. Ten-year-old Tad Lincoln climbed into the carriage with his father and Connecticut Senator L.F.S. Foster for the ride back to the Executive Mansion. Walt Whitman, among the spectators along the avenue, reported: "There were no soldiers, only a lot of civilians on horse-back, with huge yellow scarfs over their shoulders, riding around the carriage."

Two companies of Negro troops and a lodge of Negro Odd Fellows, in full regalia, were among those who marched in line, the first time that Negroes took part in the official inaugural parade. Their appearance sparked rumors that ball tickets had been sold to Negroes, a rumor that ball managers promptly denied.

A press, set upon a wagon hauled along by a local typographical society, printed a four-page issue of the *Chronicle Junior* as the procession rolled along. The unique souvenirs were distributed to eager spectators.

About three o'clock the parade was over and the city settled down until eight, when the White House gates were thrown open and several thousand persons made a grand rush to enter its portals. The Marine Band, tucked off in a side place, played fine music while the torrent of humanity streamed through the mansion and the President and Mrs. Lincoln received their guests with graceful cordiality. A guest, detained at the door by a policeman, was the former slave, noted orator, and freedom fighter Frederick Douglass. Recognizing Douglass from afar, the President called out: "Here comes my friend Douglass," and extended his hand, adding, "I am glad to see you. I saw you in the crowd today listening to my inaugural address, how did you like it?"

The National Inauguration Ball—so named because Lincoln's and the new Vice President Andrew Johnson's names had appeared at Johnson's request on the National Union, not Republican, ticket—was postponed until Monday, March 6. The beautiful great hall of the handsome, neo-classical Patent Office was the ball scene, with the American flag playing a predominant part in the decorations. There were three bands, and at ten o'clock the opening promenade started the dancing. A schedule of quadrilles, waltzes and galops, schottisches and Varsoviennes (folk dances), lanciers, and polkas followed, ending with the Virginia Reel.

The military band struck up "Hail to the Chief" after its first quadrille and President Lincoln was escorted down the center of the hall by Speaker of the House Schuyler Colfax. Mrs. Lincoln, escorted by Senator Charles Sumner, followed, wearing an elegant gown of white

Lincoln, dressed in black with a claw-hammer coat and white kid gloves, shook hands with 6000 people at the White House reception in the evening following his second inauguration. This lithograph, depicting Vice President Andrew Johnson at Lincoln's right and Mrs. Lincoln at his left side, was dedicated to Mrs. Lincoln and published by Frank Leslie's Chimney Corner *after the death of the President in 1865.*

point lace over rich white silk satin. Her jewels were pearls and her headdress was a wreath of white jessamine and purple violets. The members of the presidential party were seated on blue and gold chairs on the platform midway down the hall and crowds clustered in front of them to stare.

Soon after midnight the President and Mrs. Lincoln were ceremoniously ushered into the supper room where a spun sugar model of the Capitol centered the table. The menu was a gastronomic triumph, but the guests got out of hand. In the grand rush for food, some were seen snatching whole patés, chickens, and legs of veal and carrying them, above the heads of the cringing crowd, away for private consumption. In the midst of the orgy the Lincolns quietly left the hall, and few in the scramble for food even noticed that the President and his lady were missing. Despite its undignified supper mélée, the inauguration ball did make a contribution to one of the President's aims expressed in his inaugural address. Proceeds from the ten-dollar ball tickets were slated to go to the widows and children of men who had been killed in battle.

ANDREW JOHNSON

☆ ☆ ☆

April 15, 1865

Six weeks after his second inauguration, Abraham Lincoln was dead from an assassin's bullet and Andrew Johnson was thrust into the office of President of the United States. The Vice President himself had been spared an attempt on his life when the assassin assigned by John Wilkes Booth to kill Johnson developed cold feet and got drunk in the nearest bar. Booth, a handsome, fanatical Southern actor, shot Lincoln at Ford's Theatre on Good Friday, April 14, 1865.

A theater patron, former Wisconsin Governor Leonard Farwell, immediately walked the four blocks from Ford's to Kirkwood House, at Twelfth Street and Pennsylvania Avenue, where the Vice President was in bed. Johnson dressed and walked back with Farwell to the house across the street from the theater where the unconscious President lay dying. When Mrs. Lincoln kept her back turned to him, Johnson left quietly and returned to his hotel. A few hours later the tolling of church bells announced the tragedy. President Lincoln had died at twenty-two minutes after seven o'clock, Saturday, April 15.

Soon an urgent message from the Cabinet officers was delivered to Johnson. "By the death of President Lincoln the office of President has devolved under the Constitution upon you," the letter read. "The emergency of the Government demands that you should immediately qualify according to the requirements of the Constitution and enter upon the duties of President of the United States. If you will please make known your pleasure, such arrangements as you deem proper will be made."

Johnson replied that it would be agreeable to him to qualify himself for the high office at his Kirkwood rooms. There, to the tolling of the

Artist's conception of Andrew Johnson taking the oath of office appeared in Frank Leslie's Illustrated Newspaper.

Andrew Johnson took the oath of office prescribed for the President in his rooms at Kirkwood House, Pennsylvania Avenue at Twelfth Street.

city's church bells and the hammering of workmen tacking up black crepe on the buildings along Pennsylvania Avenue, the oath of office was administered to Andrew Johnson at eleven o'clock by Chief Justice Chase. Nearly all the Cabinet officers witnessed the simple ceremony, but Secretary of State William Seward, severely wounded in an assassination attempt the evening before—part of the Booth conspiracy—was not present.

The new President, overwhelmed by the rush of events, made a short speech, saying that he felt incompetent to perform the important duties and adding that he would rely on them "in carrying the Government through its present perils." The Cabinet officers tendered kindly greetings and were quite relieved to note that the new President looked in robust health. On an ordinary, lined piece of writing paper, someone wrote out the 35-word presidential oath which was signed by Andrew Johnson and certified by Chief Justice Chase.

Andrew Johnson may have taken the oath twice on that black Holy Saturday, according to an account related by former United States Senator from Nevada William N. Stewart shortly before his death. Stewart said that he had met the venerable Vermont Senator Solomon Foot only a few minutes after Lincoln's death, shortly after daylight, and that the two men directed the driver of a dilapidated hack to take them to the residence of Chief Justice Chase, who went back to the Kirkwood House with them. The Chief Justice administered the oath to Johnson about eight o'clock, according to this testimony. Certainly the later ceremony took place. Even in the perilous aftermath of the assassination of the President, the power of the office had passed into the hands of the rightful successor.

President Johnson was then fifty-six years old and was described by Senator J.R. Doolittle of Wisconsin as being "compact and strongly built, of dark complexion and deep set black eyes. He is of strong intellect, indomitable energy and iron will."

Andrew Johnson had been born in poverty in Raleigh, North Carolina. His father died rescuing two friends from drowning and his mother was unable to send the children to school. Andrew never attended a school for a day in his life but thirsted for knowledge and learned to read after he and his brother were apprenticed to a tailor. He later settled in Greeneville, Tennessee, and there the shoemaker's young daughter, Eliza McCardle, befriended the ambitious young tailor, taught him to write and to cipher, and married him. The self-

Andrew Johnson

made man was elected mayor, a member of the state legislature, and Governor of Tennessee before becoming United States Senator in 1857. Now, honest, stubborn Andy Johnson was President of the United States.

The new President immediately sent word to Mrs. Lincoln to stay in the White House as long as she chose and he moved in with friends. His wife was still in Tennessee. Shortly after he become President, a group of New York bankers and merchants wanted to give him an elegant carriage and span of horses. The President refused. "I am compelled solely from the conviction of duty I have ever held in deference to the acceptance of presents by those occupying high official positions to decline the offerings of kind and loyal friends," he wrote.

Andrew Johnson was the poorest man ever to become President and it seemed as though the new President was stubbornly determined to leave the White House as poor as when he entered it. And he did.

ULYSSES S. GRANT

☆ ☆ ☆

March 4, 1869   March 4, 1873

General Ulysses S. Grant was the first of the Civil War heroes to be inaugurated President, and with the Grant era there was no doubt that the age of innocence was over for the nation. At Grant's first inauguration on March 4, 1869, tickets were required for admission to the Senate Gallery, single windows overlooking the Pennsylvania Avenue parade route sold for $25.00 and $50.00 for the day, and the inaugural ball in the Treasury Building, where dancers sniffed stonecutters' dust and lost their coats in the cloakroom shuffle, was a disaster.

General Grant refused to ride in the same carriage with his predecessor, and the slighted President Johnson then declined any further part in the ceremonies. He stayed in the White House, quietly signing bills; then, at half-past twelve o'clock, as the inaugural ceremonies took place at the Capitol, Andrew Johnson bid farewell to his Cabinet members and rode off in his carriage to stay with friends.

The Fifth Cavalry escorted the President-elect's carriage along the parade route from his headquarters at Seventeenth and F Streets. Pennsylvania Avenue had been carefully scraped of accumulated dust, leaving deep ruts in the roadway which caused the carriages to rock back and forth precariously. Following the President was a procession of organized groups that included the Tanners, who took special pride in the new President because his 75-year-old father, Jesse A. Grant, present at his son's inauguration, was a leather tanner. Among the marchers were "the Invincibles, the Wide Awakes, the Grant and Colfax Clubs, and the Colored Republicans, each organization with its band, its banners, and its badges," as reported chronicler Ben Perley Poore.

Ulysses S. Grant, photographed by Matthew Brady about 1869. Note the reflector at right.

Thirty veterans of the War of 1812 were seated in one of Washington coachmaker Nailor's omnibuses, which was decorated with flags and drawn by white horses.

When 46-year-old General Grant appeared on the inaugural platform, after watching Vice President Schuyler Colfax take the oath of office in the Senate Chamber, a salute was fired from the battery in the East park and cheers went up from the crowd. Chief Justice Chase administered the oath and the cannon boomed forth twenty-one rounds in salute. Julia Dent Grant and her family proudly watched the new President, in a plain black suit, read his address in a clear but not loud voice. After the address, the procession re-formed to follow the President's carriage to the Executive Mansion, but then the gates were closed to the public and there was no reception. The President and his party watched the inaugural parade from the reviewing stand erected on Pennsylvania Avenue. As one contingent of troops passed they called out: "Three cheers for our Nellie!" to 14-year-old Nellie Grant, who was standing near her father. After the parade the Grant family returned to their I Street home to prepare for the inaugural ball.

At the Treasury, the beautiful marble room was designated as the main dancing hall and reception room, and special electric telegraph signals had been installed to call the dances in the other rooms. The President's party arrived at half-past ten and the orders were "No Hand-shaking, Gentlemen!" to the throng of five thousand.

"President Grant made an excellent impression by his unpretending simplicity, leaning lightly forward by his finger ends upon the little marble table before him and bowing his acknowledgments to the salutations of the visitors," reported *The Evening Star*. "Mrs. Grant, lady-like and unaffected, and her children's frank and unassuming style showed that they had been trained by a good mother." Mrs. Grant wore a white satin gown with a point lace cape and trim, pearl and diamond jewelry and a single japonica in her hair. Teen-age Nellie, hair flowing, wore white tulle, and her brother Fred, a West Pointer like his father, was in his cadet uniform.

While the presidential party withdrew to a private room for an elegant supper, the hoi-poloi dashed to the supper room and swept the tables clean as quickly as the astonished waiters could place food upon them. A stampede took place and the crowd burst into the kitchen

Shortly after Grant started to read his inaugural address his 14-year-old daughter, Nellie, somewhat dismayed by the excitement of the multitude, ran forward and took her father's hand. A chair was brought for her, and she sat down by the President while he finished his speech.

The supper at Grant's first inauguration ball, as seen by political cartoonist Thomas Nast.

FOURTH OF MARCH, 1873.

GENERAL U. S. GRANT'S

SECOND INAUGURATION.

ADMIT BEARER TO ANY SECTION OF SENATE GALLERY NOT RESERVED.

This card will secure admittance to the Capitol through the bronze doors of the Senate wing, which will be opened at eleven o'clock precisely.

Ticket to the Senate ceremonies at Grant's second inauguration. Admittance cards were required for the Senate gallery at an inauguration for the first time during the Grant era.

where one stout female cook succeeded in turning the tide by flipping dirty dishclothes on the ball costumes of the invaders.

Grant's second inauguration day, March 4, 1873, was the coldest ever. The temperature hovered around zero, with sleet, snow, and fierce bitter winds. The President, muffled to the ears in a dark blue beaver overcoat, with velvet collar and a high silk hat, rode to the Capitol in his own open carriage, four-in-hand. In East Capitol Park, two thousand persons shivered in the seats erected opposite the inaugural stand, which was draped with large American flags. In front was a large battle flag, riddled with scars and inscribed with the names of various battles.

The President quickly advanced to the front of the platform and there, while every head uncovered, took the oath administered by Chief Justice Chase. In the bitter cold the President read his address, the cannon roared, fire-gongs clanged, and a tremendous cheer burst forth from the spectators who had stayed the course.

On returning to the White House, President Grant took his place in the special stand erected in Lafayette Square across Pennsylvania Avenue from the White House to review the magnificently planned military parade. Valves of musical instruments stuck, several cadets in the line of march fainted from cold, and tears froze on the cheeks of

Grant passing through the rotunda of the Capitol from the Senate chamber to the inaugural platform for his re-inauguration.

First Lady Julia Dent Grant wore this gown of white and silver brocade to the 1873 inaugural ball. It is now on public display in the First Ladies Hall of the Smithsonian Institution.

the little drummer boys who proudly trooped along before the gaily decorated but deserted stands on Pennsylvania Avenue. The crowds rushed out to wave and yell for the President, then hurried back to the warmer climate of hotel rooms and hearths. That evening thousands braved the cold to view the splendid fireworks, with the finale a representation of General Grant on horseback.

But the most expensive fiasco was the grand ball in the temporary wooden wigwam built on Judiciary Square. High northerly winds whistled through the structure where the President and his party stood, shivering, on a platform at the coldest end of the room, Mrs. Grant in a dress of white and silver brocade. Most of the guests didn't part with their wraps and danced in a vain effort to keep warm.

After a tour of the room to the strains of the Naval Band's "Hail to the Chief," the President and his party were whisked into a private, warmer, supper room. In the main ballroom, men hacked away at frozen oysters, turkeys, and other luxuries that were unappealing in the frigid temperature, guests passed up champagne for hot chocolate and coffee. And overhead, canaries, imported to sing gaily for the splendid occasion, tucked their bills under their feathers and froze in their cages.

RUTHERFORD B. HAYES

☆ ☆ ☆

March 3 & 5, 1877

The dual inauguration of Rutherford Birchard Hayes on March 3 and March 5, 1877, was the climax of a high drama in the history of the republic. Never before in the nation's existence had there been a contested election with a dispute arising over which candidates were elected President and Vice President. But the electoral votes of several Southern states and Oregon had been challenged, and a special Electoral Commission was set up to count the votes and determine whether the disputed electoral votes belonged to the Democratic candidate, Governor Samuel J. Tilden of New York, or the Republican candidate, Governor Hayes of Ohio.

When Governor Hayes and his family set out from Columbus for Washington on March 1—just three days before the customary inaugural date—he remarked, good-humoredly, to the well-wishers at the railroad station that he just might be back immediately. And, indeed, it wasn't until four o'clock in the morning of March 2 in the House of Representatives that Hayes was proclaimed President of the United States with 185 votes to 184 for Tilden. Tilden's friends and political partisans were convinced that he was the rightful winner and urged him to take the office as President, peaceably if possible, forcibly if not. There were rumors that Tilden planned to take the oath on Sunday, March 4, and that two of the Supreme Court Justices considered Hayes the "usurper" and Tilden the true choice by the suffrage of the people. But Tilden, who did not question his own election, would have no part of any activities that might lead to violence.

Hayes himself was a man of honesty and strong character, dedicated

Rutherford B. Hayes

to bringing about reform and responsibility in the Republican party. He announced that he would serve as President for only one term, and did exactly that. There was little time to plan festivities to celebrate the inauguration once it was announced that the 54-year-old popular Union general was the President-elect.

On Saturday afternoon, March 3, Governor Hayes took his nine-year-old daughter, Fanny, to a matinee of the opera *Il Trovatore* and that evening, with Mrs. Hayes, he dined at the White House. While Mrs. Grant graciously mingled with her guests after dinner, the President, Chief Justice Morrison B. Waite, and the President-elect slipped into the red parlor where President Grant had arranged to have the oath of office administered to Hayes. It was the first time that an elected President was sworn into office before the day designated for taking the oath, and the first time that the country technically had two Presidents for a day. The secret ceremony was a precaution against the nation's being without a Chief Executive from noon Sunday, March 4, until noon Monday, March 5, the time slated for the inauguration at the Capitol.

On Monday morning, March 5, Representative James Garfield of

Ohio escorted President Hayes to the Executive Mansion. The two Presidents took their places, with their Congressional escort, in Grant's four-in-hand carriage. Perhaps a few spectators along the avenue noticed that Hayes was seated on the right, for he was already the President, as the carriage rolled along to the melodious strains of the Marine Band, including "Darling, I Am Growing Old." President Hayes, a handsome man with bright blue eyes and gray hair and beard, radiated joy and good health as he bowed, hat in hand, to the populace to the right and then left. Occasionally a cheer for Tilden was heard, but there was no disturbance to mar the day. Preceding the carriage was the President's

Chief Justice Morrison Waite administering the oath of office privately to Hayes at the White House, as depicted by the New York Daily Graphic *artist. At left is President Grant; at right, Secretary of State Hamilton Fish, who, however, was not present at this ceremony on March 3, 1877.*

LE MONDE ILLUSTRÉ
JOURNAL HEBDOMADAIRE

ABONNEMENTS POUR PARIS ET LES DÉPARTEMENTS

BUREAUX
13, QUAI VOLTAIRE

21ᵉ Année. Nº 1043 — 7 Avril 1877

DIRECTION ET ADMINISTRATION, 13, QUAI VOLTAIRE

The public inauguration of Hayes, at the east portico of the Capitol on March 5, 1877, was pictured on the front page of Le Monde Illustré *in Paris a month later.*

guard of honor, the Columbus Cadets, in dark blue uniforms with light blue facings, white belts and straps, and black hats with plumes of blue and white. Their drum major, in white with a towering bearskin topped by a tall cockade on his head, walked backward in front of the band.

A deafening cheer arose from the multitude at the east steps of the Capitol when the erect figure with difficulty made his way to the front of the crowded inaugural platform. A few minutes before, Vice President William A. Wheeler had taken the oath in the Senate Chamber. Chief Justice Waite administered the oath to the President, who then read his long address as Mrs. Hayes and their children watched proudly from the front row. Nearby sat an artist from an illustrated newspaper, sketching madly throughout the ceremonies. As the last words of the speech were uttered, the roar of the guns seemed to shake the hills, drums began to beat, and marching men escorted the two Presidents back to the White House. There Mrs. Grant had a sumptuous lunch prepared for the new occupants. After lunch, former President and Mrs. Grant took a kindly leave of the servants, stepped into their carriage-and-four and drove to the home of a friend.

President Hayes had accepted the invitation of the Columbus Cadets, who had gallantly come to the rescue after the election was finally decided and planned a reception honoring the President at Willard's Hotel. Escorted by General William T. Sherman, the President bowed to each cadet and ascended to the stage, where the youths were presented to him. The President then returned to the White House where Mrs. Hayes was entertaining Ohio friends in the gaslit parlors and halls.

The most spectacular event was a hastily arranged torchlight pro-

Below left: *The presidential party passes beneath the grand arch by the Treasury en route to the White House after the inauguration of Hayes.* Right: *Hayes responds to the crowds at the White House north portico in the evening, March 5, 1877.*

On March 3, 1877, the White House was the setting for an inauguration for the first time when Rutherford B. Hayes took the oath of office in a secret ceremony. This wood engraving, from a photograph by L. E. Walker, was printed in Harper's Weekly *in March, 1877.*

cession along illuminated Pennsylvania Avenue, where a gorgeous display of bunting and arches of flags spanned the parade route. Rockets were sent up throughout the march, to the delight of the lively crowd. Only four days before, such a scene would have seemed impossible. Now, despite the controversial election, the nation had a new President and, as columnist Mary Clemmer reported from Washington that day, "the world has learned anew, that a republic founded in righteousness and preserved by free government strikes far below the roots of anarchy and the storms of human passion; and, though it can be shaken, it will not be destroyed."

JAMES A. GARFIELD

☆ ☆ ☆

March 4, 1881

The mother of James A. Garfield was the first mother to witness her son's inauguration as President of the United States—on March 4, 1881. Left a poor widow when her son James was one year old, she had reared him in a log cabin and encouraged him to get a good education. Young James had worked as a tow-boy on a canal, then worked his way at Ohio's Western Reserve Eclectic Institute—later Hiram College —as the school janitor. He went on to graduate with high honors at Williams College and, at thirty-one, was the youngest brigadier general in the Union Army.

The clouds had cleared away and the sun shone brightly, melting the previous night's snow, as the President-elect read his address to the enormous crowd in front of the platform at the Capitol's east portico. Cheers punctuated the address, as they had greeted the 49-year-old President, who wore a fine black suit with a frock coat and black necktie. Closing his address, General Garfield turned toward Chief Justice Waite, who arose and stepped forward to administer the oath while Supreme Court Clerk Henry McKenney held the beautifully bound Bible.

The tall, husky, blond-bearded President turned immediately and kissed his mother. "Nobody could see it without being deeply touched, and the incident went straight to the hearts of the people," reported *Frank Leslie's Illustrated Newspaper*. Then the new President kissed his wife, Lucretia, who wore a black silk dress with a velvet basque and sat next to his mother. The Garfields' oldest daughter, Mollie, sat nearby. Former President Hayes was the first to shake General Garfield's hand

The inauguration of James Garfield, drawn by A. B. Frost for Harper's Weekly.

The Garfields open the inaugural ball in the new building of the National Museum, March 4, 1881. In the background, beneath the dome of the rotunda, a 15-foot-high statue of the Goddess of Liberty holds in her left hand a United States shield and in the right an electric torch.

and greet him as President, and then the two Ohioan Presidents were escorted from the platform to the splendid presidential carriage, which had a border of gilt around the panels.

By the time the grand procession started from the Capitol, the slush had melted and run off the fine concrete pavement that now covered Pennsylvania Avenue. The honor of serving as the President's escort went to the First Cleveland Troop, who made a handsome appearance in their French chasseur uniforms and helmets with yellow plumes. A battalion of Marines, headed by Professor John Philip Sousa and the full Marine Band, preceded the President's escort and made a fine show-ing in their colorful uniforms—dark blue coats trimmed with red, yellow epaulettes, light blue pants, and hats with yellow pompons.

President Garfield, looking a bit tired but robust, "handled his stove pipe hat with skill," reported *The Evening Star*, and as the carriage rolled through the White House gate, he rose and saluted the multitude. Then with former President Hayes by his side, he reviewed the grand procession, including a military display consisting of five divisions, from the large stand erected in front of the White House grounds, which were gaily decorated with streamers and signal flags strung from tree to tree. The columns of the north portico were draped with evergreen, and a large glass red, white, and blue star blazed with light at night in the pediment of the portico. General William T. Sherman, grand

President Garfield reviews the procession in front of the White House on Penn-sylvania Avenue. Seated at left are the President's mother and wife, at right, former President Hayes and Mrs. Hayes (in white bon-net).

marshal of the parade, did not wear his uniform but was garbed in a great coat and an army slouch hat with a gilt cord.

At eight o'clock the doors of the new National Museum building on the Smithsonian grounds were thrown open for the 5,500 inauguration ball guests who arrived by crowded streetcars and carriages. The grounds were lit by calcium, which threw dramatic shadows on the handsome buildings, and thousands of gas burners, temporarily installed especially for the ball, cast a yellowish glow through the many windows, presenting a fine spectacle in the night. "None of the numerous scenic effects of the day or evening surpassed this," noted *The Evening Star*.

The President and Mrs. Garfield, with former President and Mrs. Hayes, stood in the western hall behind a low barricade covered with red, white, and blue to receive the guests. On an arch over the door behind them was painted the United States coat of arms from which radiated the flags of all nations. By half-past ten o'clock the hand-shaking portion of the reception was suspended and the President, with Mrs. Garfield who was wearing a beautiful ball gown of rich mauve satin and Brussels point lace, designed in a graceful bustle fashion, and with bunches of pansies as her only ornamentation, led a promenade through the hall. Then they watched the brilliant scene from the balcony.

Supper was served in the temporary annex, where five hundred persons at a time could be seated to savor the feast. No wines or liquors were served, in keeping with former President Hayes's decree during his White House term. The immense ball was a brilliant success and no one dreamed that the Garfield administration would come to a crashing close only six months after its glorious beginning.

CHESTER A. ARTHUR

☆　☆　☆

September 20 & 22, 1881

At a quarter past two o'clock in the morning of September 20, 1881, as the gaslight flickered dimly in the parlor of 123 Lexington Avenue—a high-stoop brownstone house in New York City—Chester A. Arthur took the oath of office as the twenty-first President of the United States. James Garfield had died several hours before after lingering more than two months in agony from an assassin's bullets.

The 50-year-old Vice President first heard the unwanted news from a *New York Sun* reporter who arrived at the Arthur home at 11:30 P.M. and was informed at the door that General Arthur—he had been Quartermaster General of New York State during the Civil War—had received nothing later than the evening bulletin. At that moment General Arthur appeared in the hall and the reporter repeated: "The President is dead."

"Oh, no! it cannot be true. It cannot be. I have heard nothing," Arthur exclaimed. When the reporter told him that the dispatch had just been received at the *Sun* office, the stunned successor to the President replied: "I hope—my God, I do hope it is a mistake!" His voice broke at the last words, and his eyes filled with tears.

A short while later a telegram arrived. After reading it, General Arthur handed it to his friends, Elihu Root and Daniel Rollins, and buried his head in his hands. The telegram, with the formal notification of the death of the President, signed by the Cabinet, read:

"It becomes our painful duty to inform you of the death of President Garfield, and to advise you to take the oath of office as President of the United States, without delay.

"If it concurs with your judgment, we will be very glad if you will come here on the earliest train tomorrow morning."

As soon as General Arthur received the telegram, his friends who were with him at the time went out in search of a judge to administer the oath. The sound of cabs rattling up in front of the Arthur home filled the sleepy street. General Arthur's college-age son, Alan, hastened up the front steps of the house and entered the room where his father, a widower, was still too deeply affected to talk. Shortly before two o'clock, Elihu Root and Dr. R. C. Van Wyck returned with Judge John R. Brady, Justice of the New York State Supreme Court. Soon afterward, Judge Charles Donohue arrived with District Attorney Rollins and Police Commissioner Stephen French.

After the second group arrived, General Arthur led his guests from the library into the front parlor, where he stood behind a large table scattered with dispatches, books, and writing materials. Judge Brady stood facing him, with Alan Arthur and the other witnesses grouped around them. It was a striking, dramatic scene in the middle of the night. Old allegorical pictures, hanging on the walls, seemed to loom out of the dark background and the dim gaslight flickered over the white marble bust of Henry Clay.

The brownstone house at 123 Lexington Avenue, New York City, where Chester Arthur took the oath of office as President in the early morning hours of September 20, 1881.

Chester Arthur taking the oath of office at his residence in New York City. This drawing, made from life by J. W. Alexander, appeared on the cover of Harper's Weekly.

General Arthur, in a dark sack suit, had regained his composure and his fine, tall figure stood out grandly against the dark, heavy curtains that draped the large French windows. Judge Brady raised his right hand and General Arthur did likewise. Then Judge Brady administered the oath and, in a clear, ringing voice, the new President repeated it. He remained standing a moment longer with his hand still raised, and no one spoke. His teen-age son stepped forward and kissed his father gently on the cheek.

The new President, described as "a man of courtly bearing, fine dress and artistic tastes," quietly traveled to Washington on Thursday, September 22, and on his arrival there it was decided that the oath should be administered again by the Chief Justice of the United States so that it would appear in the official records of the Supreme Court.

The second ceremony, brief and impressive, was held in the private office of the Vice President in the Capitol that day, September 22. Two former Presidents—U. S. Grant and Rutherford B. Hayes—were among the witnesses. Then President Arthur, his voice trembling, read a brief address to the assembled few, who paid their respects to him as President. Meanwhile, crowds flocked to pay their respects to the late President Garfield, who lay in state in the black-draped White House.

GROVER CLEVELAND

☆ ☆ ☆

March 4, 1885

The only President who served for two terms that were not consecutive was Grover Cleveland, whose first inauguration took place on March 4, 1885. One hundred thousand strangers came to town and left one million dollars behind them when they departed after the inauguration of the first Democratic President since bachelor James Buchanan—and Cleveland, too, was a bachelor President.

The 47-year-old President-elect had served as Governor of New York and was the son of a poor Presbyterian minister who had died when the boy was sixteen. Cleveland then had to abandon his plans to attend college and became an assistant teacher in an institution for the blind. He read law and, at the age of twenty-two, was admitted to the bar with only a common school education behind him.

Cleveland—a big man, just under six feet who weighed nearly three hundred pounds—had won out over the Republican candidate, James G. Blaine. For the first time there had been a female candidate for the presidency, too, who represented the Equal Rights party. She was Belva Lockwood, a gray-haired lawyer who tricycled to her Washington law office every morning, showing a pair of well-turned ankles in red stockings as she whizzed along.

At a quarter past ten on the sunny, crisp inaugural morning, President Arthur's elegant dark green carriage, driven by veteran White House coachman Albert Hawkins, dashed up to the door of the H-Street annex of the Arlington Hotel. Out of the hotel stepped the President-elect, wearing a close-fitting Prince Albert suit with high, standing collar and black tie, dark blue overcoat, and black kid gloves. He doffed his shining

A grand illumination featuring pictures of President Grover Cleveland and Vice President Thomas Hendricks was part of the spectacular fireworks display that celebrated Cleveland's first inauguration, March 4, 1885.

beaver in response to the cheering crowds densely packed behind police lines. At the White House, President Arthur, who had entertained the bachelor President-elect and his sister, Libby, at dinner the evening before, warmly greeted him. Soon the two men entered the first carriage for the ride to the Capitol, escorted by military and civic groups and followed by a barouche carrying Vice President-elect Thomas Hendricks and Connecticut Senator Joseph Hawley.

At half-past twelve, the two Presidents and the procession of dignitaries emerged from the east door of the Capitol and moved onto the flag-draped platform. Spectators swarmed over the Capitol steps and small boys climbed into the lap of the marble statue of Washington, showing "but little reverence for the Father of His Country," as bemoaned *The Washington Post*. Before the throng of about 150,000 which had roared when he walked, bare-headed, hat in hand, down the steps, Cleveland delivered his address in a calm, solid manner, consulting his notes only occasionally. Then Chief Justice Waite administered the oath and held out a small, well-worn, leather-bound Bible which bore the inscription, "S.G. Cleveland." It had been given to him by his mother when he left home in his youth, for the new President had long since dropped his first name, Stephen. This day, in the presence of his brothers and sisters, Cleveland kissed the cherished Bible to seal his constitutional oath on becoming President.

The presidential carriage then returned to the White House where the entire party, including former President Arthur and Vice President Hendricks, joined the President in the flag-bedecked reviewing stand in front of the mansion on Pennsylvania Avenue. The most conspicuous feature of the three-hour parade was the presence of crack militia organizations from many Southern states, marching in an inaugural parade for the first time since the war, and large companies of Negroes, too.

In the evening a spectacular fireworks display was fired from the grounds south of the White House. The inaugural ball was held in the new red brick Pension Building—then unfinished—at Fifth and G Streets, Northwest, which was to be the site of inaugural balls for a quarter of a century. Three tiers of balconies overlooked the forty thousand square feet of highly waxed dance floor, and enormous ugly columns, camouflaged by beautiful decorations, trisected the floor space to the ceiling of beams and girders, concealed by a white and gold canopy. The building was well heated, lighted by bright, clear electric lights, and had ample cloak rooms.

President Cleveland led the grand march, to the music of the Marine Band conducted by the great Sousa, and the waltzes, lanciers, polkas, and promenades were kept up for nine thousand dancers until dawn. Former President Arthur delighted the crowds by attending and enjoying the ball, and the President's sister, Libby, attracted admiration in a handsome gown of white silk and lace. Vice President Hendricks, too, attended the ball which was, indeed, a fitting close to the splendid day.

BENJAMIN HARRISON

☆　☆　☆

March 4, 1889

The only grandson of a President to be inaugurated as President was Benjamin Harrison, who once declared: "I want it understood that I am the grandson of nobody. I believe that every man should stand on his own merits." But, despite his wishes, it was as the grandson of "Old Tippecanoe," William Henry Harrison, and the great grandson and namesake of a signer of the Declaration of Independence, that Benjamin Harrison was best known at his inauguration on a miserable, rainy blue Monday, March 4, 1889.

The 55-year-old Republican President-elect had won more electoral votes than the incumbent Democratic President, who had more popular votes. While President Cleveland rode to the Capitol with his successor in his open carriage, Frances Folsom Cleveland, a White House bride three years before, was giving last minute instructions in the Executive Mansion to the staff. "I want to find everything just as it is now when we come back again," she said. "We are coming back just four years from today." And they did.

On entering the carriage at the White House for the ride to the Capitol, President-elect Harrison sat down on the right side, traditionally the seat of the President, and there was some confusion as they scrambled about before both men were properly seated. Then the President took an umbrella, handed to him by an usher, and held it over them both. In the opposite seat were Missouri Senator Francis Cockrell and Massachusetts Senator George Hoar, struggling to raise an umbrella which promptly collapsed. Secretary of the Treasury Charles Fairchild,

117

standing nearby, was raising his umbrella when the President spotted him and said:

"Fairchild, lend us your umbrella?" The reluctant Secretary handed it to Senator Cockrell and the President laughed and said: "We're honest folks, we'll bring it back!" "I don't know about that," Secretary Fairchild replied as the carriage rolled off, the President and two Senators laughing heartily while "General Harrison smiled behind his beard and continued putting on his gloves," as noted *The Evening Star*.

With President Cleveland holding the umbrella over General Harrison's head on the wind-swept platform at the east portico of the Capitol, the President-elect took the oath administered by Chief Justice Melville W. Fuller before a rain-soaked but enthusiastic crowd. Those lucky enough to be directly in front of the inaugural platform were the wettest, for as soon as a man put up an umbrella, blocking the view, it was promptly smashed. By the time President Harrison had finished reading the typewritten copy of his address, no more than four thousand spectators remained. The new Vice President, Levi P. Morton, had been sworn into office in the warm, dry Senate Chamber.

Many of the veterans of Harrison's old Seventieth Indiana Regiment who marched up to the Capitol and back again, soaked to the skin, as personal escort to their old commander, were white-haired men. Afterward they suffered a number of deaths in their ranks which were directly attributed to the chilling march.

From the reviewing stand in front of the White House the President watched the water-logged parade of military. The colorful chief marshal was handsome, one-legged General James Beaver, Governor of Pennsylvania, who was strapped to his horse and rode the avenue, hat in hand, with rain dripping down his neck. Buffalo Bill and his Wild West troop attracted cheers, too.

But the rain did nothing to dampen the enthusiasm for the inaugural

Souvenir mugs featured portraits of both Benjamin Harrison and George Washington because the centennial celebration commemorating the first inauguration took place during the Harrison inaugural year, 1889.

The inauguration of Benjamin Harrison at the east portico of the Capitol, March 4, 1889.

ball, when twelve thousand persons crowded into the Pension Building for the brilliant event. The Marine Band's great conductor Sousa had composed a "Presidential Polonaise" especially for the ball, and dancers dined on oysters served several ways, turkey, chicken, lobster salad, and paté de foie gras, among other dishes, but no wines or punch were served.

The President and his party arrived at ten o'clock, and both First Lady Caroline Scott Harrison and their daughter, Mary Harrison McKee, wore gowns that were memorably beautiful and of American manufacture. Mrs. Harrison's was of silver-gray silk, featuring a design taken from Indiana bur oaks, and was trimmed with gold and silver beads, with fringe outlining the apricot silk-edged panels of the skirt; while her daughter's dress was brocaded with a goldenrod design, the President's favorite flower. Mrs. McKee's dress was fashioned of parchment-colored satin, old gold taffeta, and apple-green velvet in an elaborate bustle style and was trimmed with amber and silver beads.

GROVER CLEVELAND

☆ ☆ ☆

March 4, 1893

Grover Cleveland's second inauguration on March 4, 1893, took place in the midst of a snowstorm. At the Capitol, while Vice President Adlai Stevenson took the oath in ceremonies in the Senate Chamber, a guard of Capitol policemen stretched in front of the bronze doors to keep eager spectators from the outdoor inaugural platform, and as soon as the guard dispersed there was a pell-mell rush for places near the President.

As a dainty, pretty lady appeared in the doorway and started down the aisle, wearing a blue cloak and a little bonnet trimmed with black lace and white and yellow ribbons with egret feathers, a great shout went up. It was the fair young Mrs. Cleveland, who, having endeared herself to the American people as a White House bride, now returned, at twenty-eight with a baby daughter, to the White House as the undisputed First Lady of the land.

In the cold, blustering northwest wind, Cleveland stood bareheaded to take the oath, again on his mother's Bible, administered by Chief Justice Fuller. Then he delivered his simple, direct address in a manly way and, the ceremony over, returned to the White House. There the President stood for five hours to review the parade that passed in the snowstorm.

In the evening came the handsomest inauguration ball that Washington had ever seen, when the great columns of the Pension Building were covered with ivy and the splashing water of the fountain, a bower of green, was lighted by colored electric lights. "Myriads of electric lights— the perfection of Edison's genius—sparked in every nook and corner,"

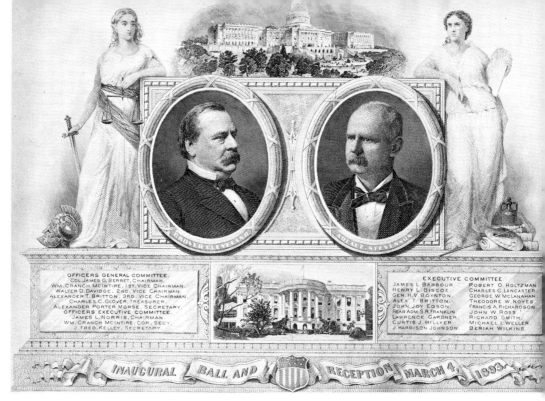

Souvenir of the inaugural ball honoring Cleveland and Vice President Adlai Stevenson, March 4, 1893.

Stands along the inaugural parade route fill with snow as the grand procession honoring Cleveland's second inauguration moves up Pennsylvania Avenue.

First Lady Frances Folsom Cleveland

reported *The New York Herald.* "On a huge electric fan . . . a red democratic spider chased the little republican fly around his web."

About half-past nine the President and Mrs. Cleveland arrived and the President, entering first on the arm of General John Schofield, was heartily cheered. But when "Frankie," as she was affectionately known, Cleveland was recognized, the crowd went wild and let out an euthusiastic yell. The First Lady wore a gown of blue-white satin trimmed with crystal jets and old rosepoint lace, and across the bodice were looped ropes of diamonds. On her head she wore a rose coronet of diamonds. Over her gown was a tan cloth wrap capped by a full ermine cape.

The Presidential party walked slowly up the stairs to the strains of "The Great Republic," composed by Marine Band leader Francisco Fanciulli for the occasion. In the south gallery, rooms had been transformed into flowery bowers for the presidential party, and there Mrs. Cleveland stayed, to the disappointment of the crowd that clustered at the stairs. The President descended to open the ball by making one tour of the dance floor, and there was more promenading than dancing throughout the evening. At midnight, the ball was over. Mrs. Cleveland, the most popular lady in America, had, noted *The Herald*, "cleverly escaped the very reputable mobbing which she feared."

WILLIAM McKINLEY

☆　☆　☆

March 4, 1897　　March 4, 1901

William McKinley was the first President to have his inauguration captured in motion pictures, copyrighted by Thomas Alva Edison, and also to have his inaugural address recorded as he gave it on March 4, 1897. An enterprising Washington amusement-hall owner then had the address installed in his entertainment gallery where, by dropping a nickel in a slot, listeners could hear the President speak on a gramophone record.

The 54-year-old Republican was the last of the Civil War Presidents, and the survivors of his old regiment—the Twenty-third Ohio—many of them now aged—had the place of honor behind their Major McKinley's carriage on the beautiful day. As McKinley left his hotel, Ebbitt House, for the White House, the handsome, yellow-plumed Black Horse Troop from Cleveland clattered along beside the carriage as special escort to the Ohio President-elect.

At the White House, President Cleveland finished signing bills before the two men entered the President's carriage for the ride to the Capitol. While photographers delayed their departure, Mrs. Cleveland stood smiling down from an upper window of the mansion. McKinley saw her, raised his hat gallantly, and bowed just as the open landau, drawn by four handsome horses with silver-mounted harnesses, started to roll away. Mrs. Cleveland smilingly waved her handkerchief.

The inaugural ceremonies took place on a low platform running along the east front of the Capitol, from the northeast corner of the Senate to the center of the building. Near the extreme right was a raised platform, enclosed with a red- and blue-covered railing, with a

*President William McKinley kisses the Bible after taking the oath of office,
March 4, 1897. Former President Cleveland is at right, Chief Justice Melville
Fuller with back to camera.*

mammoth national shield directly in front. There McKinley and Chief
Justice Fuller stood face to face, with President Cleveland at McKinley's
side. The clerk of the Supreme Court stepped forward with a large,
morocco-bound Bible that had been presented to McKinley by the
Negro bishops of the African Methodist Episcopal Church. With his
right hand raised, and holding his hat in his left, McKinley repeated the
oath slowly and impressively, then reverently kissed the open book.
Once more the government had changed hands with dignity, and former
President Cleveland extended his right hand in congratulation.

Seated nearby, beaming with pride, were the President's wife and his
84-year-old, black-clad mother. Ida Saxton McKinley, the President's
sweet-faced, blue-eyed wife, wore blue velvet trimmed with Valen-

ciennes with a matching bonnet and cape. She had been an invalid since losing, within three years, her mother and two baby daughters. Ever since she had suffered from epilepsy and led a quiet, retiring life. At any public affair, her husband had her at his side, regardless of precedent, rank, or tradition. He cared for her with a kindness and patience that were remarkable, to the day he was mortally wounded.

The President—a handsome, suave figure—read his address in ringing tones. Among the colorful guests in town was former Queen Liliuo-kalani of the Hawaiian Islands, who had watched from the diplomatic gallery in the Senate while Garret A. Hobart was sworn in as Vice President.

The two Presidents were escorted through cheering crowds along the avenue back to the White House where they stepped into the oval Blue Room for a few moments of private conversation. Then former President Cleveland stepped into his carriage and was driven to the Seventh Street wharf where a tender, with steam up, waited to take him down the Potomac on a fishing holiday.

After luncheon in the State Dining Room, President McKinley watched the parade on the avenue from a glass-enclosed reviewing stand, with a sliding front, for almost three hours. He greeted each contingent in the parade with the same graciousness, reported the *New York Herald*. "Off came the tall hat with a sweeping gesture, forward bent the body in a graceful, welcoming obeisance, a bright smile lighted up the stern, almost melancholy features and the whole demeanor of the man seemed to say:—'Thank you, my friends. I am not your President; I am your fellow worker. God bless you, and come again.'" A platoon of tandem bicycle wheelmen rode by, with rifles swinging from straps, and a fun-loving group of Marines paraded along with a goat called "Major" in the lead.

For the grand ball, the courtyard of the Pension Building was decorated in shades of white and gold, in keeping with the Republican promise to maintain the gold standard, and new frosted light bulbs gave a softened glow that transformed the prosaic building into an Arabian Nights' palace. The most popular feature was the music, furnished by Haley's Orchestra and the Gilmore Band, now under the new direction of Victor Herbert and better than ever.

The President and Vice President with their wives attended the ball, where three flower-bedecked rooms were reserved for them. Exhausted by the excitement and activity of the great day, Mrs. McKinley col-

President McKinley delivers his second inaugural address, March 4, 1901.

lapsed while standing in the great ballroom and fell. The President, in his usual, gentle way, quietly took her home for their first night in the White House.

At McKinley's second inauguration there was a new Vice President—Theodore Roosevelt, who had resigned as Secretary of War to help form a regiment of United States Volunteers known as the Rough Riders during the brief Spanish-American War. As Colonel "Teddy" Roosevelt, who led the famous charge of San Juan Hill in Cuba to win the war, TR was a popular hero. Rough Rider hats were being hawked with other souvenirs—portraits of President McKinley and Puerto Rican dolls—along Pennsylvania Avenue on March 4, 1901.

It was raining—a cold, driving rain that even blew under the pagoda-like inaugural stand—when the presidential party emerged from the Capitol after the brief ceremonies when Vice President Roosevelt took the oath of office. As soon as the President arrived, Mrs. McKinley, who had witnessed the ceremony in the Senate Chamber, was escorted from the rainswept stand and back to the White House. Then at 1:17 P.M. President McKinley repeated the oath in clear tones after Chief Justice Fuller and kissed a small, opened Bible to begin his second term. It was pouring, and the enormous flags that formed a red, white, and blue backdrop "hung like wet clothes upon the line," reported *The Washington Post*.

After the inaugural address, the President and Vice President were honored at an informal luncheon in a Senate committee room before the glittering procession, centered by a simply dressed man in a plain carriage, returned along Pennslyvania Avenue to the White House. It was exactly one hundred years since Thomas Jefferson had taken the oath of office as third President of the United States, the first inaugurated in Washington.

Swarthy Puerto Rican soldiers, wearing the uniform of the United States, were among those who passed the President's reviewing stand in the parade. It was the first time in the nation's history that an American dependency was represented in the inaugural tribute to the President.

The courtyard ballroom glittered in golden splendor in the Pension Building that evening, jammed by twelve thousand ballgoers. The President and Mrs. McKinley arrived a few minutes before ten o'clock and led the way to their second-floor suite. But the grand promenade had been left out of the program because the President did not want to weary the First Lady, who wore a white satin and lace gown featuring a scalloped circular skirt with a full train. With it she wore a diamond necklace, fitted over the high collar, and white satin shoes, modeled like ordinary walking boots except for the pearl embroidery trim. At the splendid midnight supper Mrs. McKinley led the way, escorted by her husband and General Nelson Miles. Then, after watching the scene below on the dance floor which delighted them both, the President and First Lady departed shortly before one o'clock.

The courtyard of the Pension Office, site of inaugural balls from Cleveland to Taft, sparkled with thousands of electric lights for McKinley's second inaugural ball.

THEODORE ROOSEVELT

☆ ☆ ☆

September 14, 1901   March 4, 1905

Theodore Roosevelt, at forty-two, was the youngest man ever to become President of the United States. He succeeded to the office on September 13, 1901, when President McKinley died eight days after being shot by an assassin at the Pan American Exposition in Buffalo, New York.

A special messenger with a telegram informing him that the President was worse reached the Vice President just below the summit of Mount Marcy in the Adirondacks, where he had hiked with a guide. Colonel Roosevelt hurried down the mountain, got a wagon, and drove over rough, storm-washed roads in the black of night to the nearest railway station. By one-thirty the following afternoon, Saturday, September 14, he left the train at Buffalo's Terrace Station where he was met by George L. Williams, with his private carriage, Ansley Wilcox, and a detachment of Signal Corps and a platoon of mounted police. The heavily escorted carriage returned to the Wilcox residence, where Roosevelt had been a houseguest a few days before, and there he ordered the Signal Corps and police discharged.

After lunch Colonel Roosevelt drove, with Wilcox, to the John Milburn residence where President McKinley had died. Mrs. McKinley was unable to see visitors, and Roosevelt talked to members of the late President's Cabinet. They had already made arrangements for an immediate oath-taking ceremony and told Roosevelt that they hoped he would meet their wishes. He agreed and was driven back to the Wilcox residence. There the Cabinet assembled in the library with Roosevelt, who, noticing that only three newspaper representatives were present,

The Ansley Wilcox home in Buffalo, New York, site of the brief ceremony on September 14, 1901, in which Theodore Roosevelt took the oath of office following the death of William McKinley.

instructed his host, Wilcox, to invite the other newspapermen inside, too.

For the second time in his life, Secretary Root stood by the side of a Vice President taking the oath of office upon the assassination of a President. He broke down as he started to say "Mr. Vice President," and, regaining his voice, he said, with tears trickling down his cheeks, "I have been requested by all the members of the Cabinet of the late President who are present in the City of Buffalo, all except two, to request that for reasons of weight affecting the administration of the Government you should proceed to take the constitutional oath of office as President of the United States."

Roosevelt's eyes were moist and his voice wavered at first, growing stronger as he replied: "I shall take the oath at once in accord with the request of you members of the Cabinet, and in this hour of our deep and terrible national bereavement I wish to state that it shall be my aim to continue absolutely unbroken the policy of President McKinley for the peace, the prosperity and the honor of our beloved country."

He turned toward Judge John R. Hazel of the United States District Court for the Western District of New York, who said: "Theodore Roosevelt, raise your right hand."

Then Judge Hazel read the constitutional oath, written on a sheet of parchment. Roosevelt repeated the phrases after him, and Judge Hazel added: "And thus you swear."

Rough Riders on horseback and Secret Servicemen on foot form a complete bodyguard and escort for Theodore Roosevelt's carriage on the way to the Capitol, March 4, 1905.

"And thus I swear," echoed Theodore Roosevelt in this simple yet impressive ceremony. There was no Bible used. Of the fifty-odd witnesses present, about one-half were newspaper men.

The new President's right hand and chin lowered simultaneously, and the silence was unbroken for a minute that seemed like a silent prayer. Then, at Judge Hazel's request, the new President wrote "Theodore Roosevelt" in a strong hand at the bottom of the oath on parchment.

After a brief meeting with the Cabinet, the President walked down the block with Secretary Root, then returned to the Wilcox home for a quiet dinner with the Wilcox family. The nation had a new Chief Executive, or, as Senator Mark Hanna said: "Now that damned cowboy is President of the United States!"

Theodore Roosevelt had, indeed, been a cowboy, and he was proud of it. The son of a wealthy, aristocratic New York family, he had been a sickly child who suffered from asthma and nearsightedness. Determined to build up his physique, he did so first by exercising at home, then by leading "the strenuous life" in everything he tackled, from wrestling to big game hunting. When he was twenty-five, both his mother and his lovely young wife, Alice, died coincidentally on the same day, and the griefstricken young man, a Harvard graduate, headed West and took up ranching in the Badlands of the Dakotas. There his daily companions were cowboys as they rode the range together. Roosevelt was a nature lover and an early champion of conservation, deploring the wanton destruction of natural forests.

From the men of the Western plains came many of the recruits for the Rough Riders. When Roosevelt led them in the celebrated charge of San Juan Hill in 1897, he galvanized a group of instant heroes for the American public. Almost eight years later, a loyal band of Rough Riders arrived in Washington to be the personal escort for their beloved Colonel Roosevelt at his inauguration as President.

The gala Roosevelt inauguration on March 4, 1905, was, indeed, a triumph for TR had been elected President in his own right. The only thing lacking to make the victory celebration complete was, according to the President's spirited 21-year-old daughter Alice, the defeated

Theodore Roosevelt reviews his inaugural parade in front of the White House, March 4, 1905. Mrs. Roosevelt is seated at right, front row.

The Corps of Cadets from the Carlisle Indian School passing the White House in the inaugural parade for Theodore Roosevelt, preceded by Indian Chiefs Quanah Parker of the Comanches, Little Plume of the Nez Percé, Buckskin Charlie of the Utes, Hollow Horn Bear of the Sioux, Geronimo of the Apaches, and American Horse of the Sioux.

Democratic candidate "marching in chains." Despite this omission, the inaugural parade was the most colorful the capital had even seen. Anthracite coal miners, in their miners' hats, marched in honor of the man who had settled the anthracite coal strike. Indian chiefs, including the old Apache warrior Geronimo, rode horseback. The President's neighbors from Oyster Bay, New York, were eagerly greeted by the Roosevelt youngtsers, Kermit and Ethel. Cowboys yelled as they rode by the reviewing stand—and the President yelled back, waving his hat—and Negro Cavalry troopers brought from the President the exclamation: "Ah, they were with me at Santiago." Bands played "There'll Be a Hot Time in the Old Town Tonight" and "Dixie," and the President kept time with his hand as he watched the parade for over three hours from his box in the elaborate Court of History, constructed on Pennsylvania Avenue between Fifteenth and Seventeenth Streets. There statues of famous historical Americans that had been imported from abroad originally for the St. Louis fair lined the avenue.

As the last of the 35,000 men passed by, at a quarter past six, the President remarked: "It was a great success. Bully. And did you note that bunch of cowboys? Oh, they are the boys who can ride. It all was superb. It really touched me to the heart."

The inaugural ceremonies at the Capitol had taken place at noon on the beautiful clear day. The President took the oath, administered by Chief Justice Fuller on the platform at the east portico, wearing an opal ring that had been Lincoln's. The ring was loaned to him by Secretary of State John Hay, who had been Lincoln's private secretary. Then the President gave his address in which he promised to "give everyone a square deal—no more and no less." TR's buoyancy and electric energy were contagious, firing the enthusiasm of the battalions of Americans who swarmed over the Capitol and grounds.

First Lady Edith Kermit Roosevelt, TR's second wife, had invited Mrs. Charles Fairbanks, the wife of the new Vice President, to sit by her in the inaugural stand. At the conclusion of the address, Mrs. Roosevelt hurried back to the White House where an informal luncheon was served to the Cabinet and a few invited guests.

The inauguration of Theodore Roosevelt, March 4, 1905, at the east portico of the Capitol.

First Lady Edith Kermit Roosevelt's inaugural ball gown was fashioned of robin's egg blue brocade, designed with pinwheels of gold ostrich feathers, woven especially for her by a Paterson, New Jersey, mill. Heirloom rose point lace formed the bertha at the square neckline.

The President had invited his Rough Rider escort and the officers of his personal escort, Squadron A of New York, to a five o'clock White House luncheon, but it had to begin without the President, who was still reviewing the parade, though he entered in time to greet his guests. Upon their departure, he stood on the steps of the north portico to receive a delegation of Harvard students, in their caps and gowns, and a group of cowboys on their ponies. It was seven o'clock, and dark, as the cowboys clattered up, half-halting their ponies as they leaned over to shake hands with the President, who greeted many familiarly by name.

At the inaugural ball in the Pension Building, the President and First Lady, and Vice President and Mrs. Fairbanks made a promenade in a roped-off path around the ballroom floor, with two Secret Servicemen in evening clothes immediately following the President. Then the President held an informal reception in his private room before viewing the ball from his box. "Princess Alice," in a beautiful gown of gold gauze and white satin, with pink roses scattered on the train, waved and called to her friends, as her father was doing, until, she later reported, the President firmly told her to sit down.

At the private supper, served at nine round tables centered by the President's, among the guests were the President's orphaned niece, Eleanor, and her fiancé, a distant cousin, Franklin D. Roosevelt. It was eleven-thirty when the President and First Lady left their rose-bedecked box and were escorted safely back to the White House.

WILLIAM HOWARD TAFT

☆ ☆ ☆

March 4, 1909

William Howard Taft, a distinguished jurist who longed to be a Supreme Court Justice, was inaugurated as President on March 4, 1909, during a raging blizzard that forced the ceremonies to be held in the Senate Chamber of the Capitol. The hale and hearty President-elect, who stood more than six feet and weighed more than three hundred pounds, agreed to have the inauguration of an elected President held indoors, for the first time in seventy-six years, only when reminded that it would be cruel to compel the aged Chief Justice Fuller to stand outside in the bitter weather.

The capital was isolated by the fierce storm which had raged during the night, cutting off all telegraph and telephone communications with other cities and humiliating the weatherman, who had predicted fair weather for the inauguration. Railroads were paralyzed, some trains limping in eight hours late from Baltimore. Thousands arrived in Washington after the parade was over. Fortunately, Mrs. Roosevelt had invited the Tafts to spend the night of March 3 in the White House. After dinner, while the President went to his office, Taft went to the New Willard Hotel to spend his last evening as a private citizen at a smoker given by his classmates of the Yale Class of '78.

The next morning when Taft came down to breakfast he remarked to the President: "I always said it would be a cold day when I got to be President of the United States." Promptly at ten o'clock the party left the White House, Roosevelt shaking hands with the staff members at the door, bidding them, "Goodbye and good luck." He planned to go directly from the Capitol to Union Station and take the train for Oyster

Theodore Roosevelt and William H. Taft drive to the Capitol, March 4, 1909.

Bay. The President and President-elect, with their Senate escort, entered Roosevelt's own closed carriage, drawn by four splendid bays, which rolled out the White House drive, followed by two carriages bearing Vice President Fairbanks, Vice President-elect John Sherman, and their Congressional escorts. The new President's personal escort was Troop A, National Guard of Ohio.

As the President's carriage turned into Fifteenth Street by the Treasury Building it was greeted by applause from the spectators who had cheerfully endured the sharp wind and blinding snow for this moment. Roosevelt leaned out of the window and waved his hand while Taft leaned forward within the carriage and smiled. The Black Horse Troop from Cleveland fell in behind as escort. Helen Herron Taft was driven in a "limousine" automobile to the Capitol, while Mrs. Roosevelt departed from the White House, eventually to board the train.

At the Capitol Mrs. Taft met her relatives and guests, including her three children—Robert, Helen, and Charles. The youngest, 11-year-old Charlie, had brought along a copy of *Treasure Island* to read if he got bored while his father delivered his inaugural address.

In the Senate Chamber, Taft and TR sat side by side in high-backed

TR and Taft climb the Capitol steps for Taft's inauguration.

chairs while Vice President Fairbanks administered the oath to Vice President Sherman, who then solemnly announced that the Chief Justice would administer the oath to the President-elect. Taft rose and was escorted up the steps on the right leading to the dais of the Vice President. Simultaneously, the venerable Chief Justice was escorted up the left steps and there, directly back of the Vice President's desk, the two men met. With his right hand raised, Taft repeated the oath in a firm, strong voice, following the Chief Justice's feeble tones. The new, 51-year-old President, a Unitarian, then kissed the Supreme Court Bible, held by the Chief Justice. Taft was destined to take another oath on this Bible a dozen years later—that of Chief Justice of the Supreme Court of the United States.

As the outbursts of applause and shouts of "Hurrah for Taft!" greeted him, the President fumbled nervously with his glasses, finally relaxing to show the famous Taft smile. At the conclusion of his address, the former President bounded forward to shake his hand and the two chatted warmly for a few moments before Roosevelt dashed from the chamber, stealing the show as the crowd cheered the departing idol. At the eastern portico, the President was joined by Mrs. Taft who, wearing a stunning purple satin ensemble, made history as she stepped into the carriage. She was the first President's wife to ride with her husband from the Capitol to the White House after his inauguration, and she loved every minute of it. The storm had abated and the Tafts rode with the top down on their carriage, despite the frigid weather, to the delight of the crowds that clustered along the avenue.

While the First Lady entertained luncheon guests, the President skipped lunch and walked to the stand in the Court of Honor to review the three-hour parade. The band played "Home Sweet Home" when the Citizens' Taft Club of Cincinnati passed the stand, and tears overflowed from the President's eyes, but quickly changed to smiles when they broke into song with "Bill, Bill, we'll have four good years of Bill." At five o'clock, the President and Mrs. Taft entertained the Yale Class of '78 at tea, and then the President was entertained by his classmates at dinner at the Metropolitan Club.

The brilliance of the ball in the Pension Building made up for the miserable weather that had marred the day. The Presidential party made a promenade through the ballroom, with members of the ball committee holding a red, white, and blue silk rope to mark the path of the line of march. They held a reception in their private rooms before entering the

The snowstorm over, the President and First Lady leave the Capitol after the inauguration. Mrs. Taft made history as the first President's wife to ride with her husband in the procession from the Capitol to the White House.

The beautiful inaugural ball gown worn by First Lady Helen Herron Taft was fashioned of white silk chiffon which Mrs. Taft had sent to Tokyo to be embroidered in a goldenrod pattern outlined by crystal beads and silver thread. Mrs. Taft's ball gown was the first dress presented to the Smithsonian Institution for its Collection of Dresses of the First Ladies of the White House and is now on display to the public in the First Ladies Hall of the Smithsonian Museum of History and Technology, Washington.

presidential box, where the President and First Lady received a rousing ovation. Then they stepped back and gave the place of honor to the Vice President and Mrs. Sherman, which endeared the jovial President and his wife even more to the crowd. There was a seated supper at eleven-thirty, and after a last lingering view from the presidential box, the President and Mrs. Taft together with their children left the ball shortly before one o'clock in the morning.

WOODROW WILSON

☆ ☆ ☆

March 4, 1913   March 4 & 5 1917

"This is not a day of triumph; it is a day of dedication," Woodrow Wilson told the throng that gathered at the east portico of the Capitol to cheer his inaugural speech on a delightfully warm March 4, 1913. But for the Democrats, who hadn't inaugurated a President in twenty years, it was, indeed, a day of triumph. The South shared in the celebrations of the day, too, for Andrew Johnson had been the last President from a Southern state until the Virginia-born Wilson, whose home was now in New Jersey, took the oath of office from an old Confederate soldier, Chief Justice Edward D. White.

Accompanied by students from Princeton University, where he had been both professor and president before serving as governor of New Jersey, the 56-year-old Wilson arrived in Washington on March 3 while five thousand suffragettes were marching along Pennsylvania Avenue carrying banners like bayonets. Some bore legends: "Votes for Women" and "Equal Rights." On one float sat the blind and deaf Helen Keller, a lonely figure in white looking like a statue, and the avenue blossomed with small yellow flags—the suffrage color. The President-elect gallantly made a detour and drove by a roundabout way from the station to his hotel where he waited until the spectacular suffragette parade was over before calling at the White House on President Taft.

The next day a group of Princeton students followed Wilson as he entered the White House grounds to join Taft for the ride to the Capitol. When the President-elect stepped from his carriage the students started to sing college songs, and Wilson, deep in thought, walked into the mansion, then turned and retraced his steps to the front portico.

An old man approaches the carriage to speak to Wilson and Taft at the Capitol on March 4, 1913, as spectators, including some in trees, watch.

There he stood, hat in hand and visibly moved, until the Princeton serenade was over.

The two Presidents took their places in an open landau and, to the blare of trumpets, moved off, followed by Vice President-elect Thomas R. Marshall's carriage. A guard of honor from the crack Essex Troop of Newark, New Jersey, rode beside the Presidential carriage while the mounted cadets from the Culver Military Academy of Indiana smartly brought up the rear of the six-carriage procession. President Taft, who had lost the three-way election, was as popular with the crowds as was the slender, scholarly winner by his side, for Taft's good nature and hearty smile brought cheers for "a darn good loser."

Cadets from Annapolis and West Point, including Dwight D. Eisenhower of Abilene, Kansas, paraded in front of the President's platform at the Capitol, keeping the crowd back out of hearing distance. Noticing the situation, President Taft sent word that the troops be moved to let the people come nearer to hear the address of President Wilson, who simultaneously waved his arms and called, "Let the people come in."

A quarter of a million visitors lined the parade route and gave a continuous ovation to the two Presidents on their return trip after the ceremonies. At the White House First Lady Ellen Axson Wilson, who had taken a short cut back from the Capitol, greeted guests in the State Dining Room where the two men arrived for a hasty luncheon at 2:40 P.M. Then the former President left to meet Mrs. Taft at the train bound for Augusta, Georgia, and President Wilson walked to the box in the Court of Honor to review the most magnificent military pageant in the capital's history. A French lecturer, André de Fouquieres, in the crowd, noted that Americans did not follow the custom of lifting their hats when the flag passed, "Yet I saw President Wilson saluting the flag alone with a noble and impressive gesture," he wrote in *The New York Times*.

Guests joined the President and First Lady on the south portico to watch the fireworks display on the ellipse after an early family dinner. A ball had been planned, but it was vetoed by the President who considered the solemnity of the inauguration not in keeping with the frivolity of a ball. Then the President, accompanied by one of his daughters, attended a dinner given by Princeton alumni at the Shoreham Hotel for about an hour.

Later, back at the White House, bells summoned a doorkeeper to the suite where the President needed a trunk that had gone astray. The

First Lady Edith Bolling Galt Wilson accompanies her husband to his re-inauguration, March 5, 1917.

President Wilson delivers his inaugural address at the Capitol, March 5, 1917.

trunk arrived, in the early morning hours, long after the weary President had gone to bed.

For the fourth time in the nation's history, the traditional inauguration day of March 4 fell on Sunday in 1917. It was a time of international crisis, for the United States had severed diplomatic relations with Germany, which was already at war with Great Britain and France. The nation should not be without a President for a day, it was decided, so Wilson quietly slipped to the Capitol on Sunday and there, in the President's room, the constitutional oath was privately administered by Chief Justice White.

The next day, March 5, was clear and cold. Secret Servicemen closed in around the President's open landau on Pennsylvania Avenue, which was lined by bronzed soldiers fresh from duty on the Mexican border. Armed detectives were stationed on roof tops along the avenue, and machine guns had been placed in the Capitol Plaza. The most elaborate precautions to guard the President had been taken since Lincoln's first inauguration. On the ride to the Capitol the President was accompanied by his second wife, the former Edith Bolling Galt, whom he had married after the death of the first Mrs. Wilson in 1915.

A scene during the 1917 inaugural parade. Five weeks later, the United States entered the World War.

Again the President took the oath, this time on the inaugural platform at the east portico. He kissed the Bible, which had also been used when he was sworn in as Governor of New Jersey, gave his address, and was escorted with Mrs. Wilson back to the White House.

While their luncheon guests took their time in the State Dining Room, the President and First Lady took their seats in the comfortable, glass-enclosed, heated reviewing stand. There were 25,000 men in the procession, but the most oustanding contingent was a group of women—the first women ever to take part in an inaugural parade. Mrs. Wesley Martin Sonter of Washington, carrying a large American flag, was escorted by five women on horseback, and about one hundred others, from Southern and Western states that had granted women the right to vote, marched behind, carrying a large banner proclaiming: "We did it—the West and the South." Also marching in the procession, with difficulty, were a handful of Civil War veterans carrying a banner in the stiff breeze. It read: "G.A.R. Ready for Duty." Five weeks later, the nation was at war.

WARREN G. HARDING

☆ ☆ ☆

March 4, 1921

Warren Gamaliel Harding was the first President of the United States to ride to his inauguration in an automobile, on March 4, 1921. The 55-year-old Republican had requested that the inaugural ceremonies be of the simplest character, and so they were. His wishes were motivated by his concern for his stricken predecessor, Woodrow Wilson, who had to be assisted into the automobile by Secret Servicemen at the White House. The motorcar, escorted by cavalry, was followed by Vice President Marshall, Vice President-elect Calvin Coolidge, and two members of the inaugural committee in the second car.

It was a brilliant, crisp day and Pennsylvania Avenue was ablaze with colorful decorations, but there were comparatively few spectators watching the open car bearing the two Presidents, who seemed to be holding a deep conversation on their way to the Capitol. Actually, the two men were discussing animals and Harding was telling the President the true story of a faithful elephant that was remarkably devoted to his Indian keeper. Enemies declared that the handsome Harding had been elected by women, now granted the vote nationwide by the Nineteenth Amendment which Wilson had signed into law less than three months before the election.

When the car arrived at the Capitol, the President's condition was dramatically emphasized when President-elect Harding with Senator Philander Knox and Speaker of the House "Uncle Joe" Cannon alighted and mounted the Senate steps. The President, unable to walk up the steps with his successor, was driven to a side door where he was lifted

President Wilson, left, and President-elect Warren Harding drive to the Capitol on inauguration day, March 4, 1921, with their Congressional escort, Speaker of the House Joseph Cannon (left, front seat) and Senator Philander Knox.

out of the car. Then, with great effort, he grasped his cane and limped slowly to the elevator. He went to the President's room, signed a few bills, and greeted Senators and Cabinet members. But the President, a stroke victim, was too fatigued to attend the inaugural ceremonies. While he was being driven to his new home at 2340 S Street, Northwest, Harding was watching the ceremonies in the Senate Chamber, where Calvin Coolidge took the oath as Vice President and gave his inaugural address.

At the east portico of the Capitol, the President took the oath with one hand on the open Bible which had been used at Washington's first inauguration. Standing in the small pavilion, designed after Corinthian architecture, erected over the steps, Harding repeated the oath slowly and clearly after Chief Justice White, then bent over to kiss the Bible, and lifted his head smiling. The Marine Band, smartly attired in scarlet coats and bright blue trousers, struck up "The Star Spangled Banner" in front of the kiosk, and the crowd cheered.

As President Harding delivered his address, an amplifier, hidden by the flag that covered the ceiling of the kiosk, carried his words to the outermost persons in the throng at the Capitol. Vice President Coolidge was the first to shake hands with the President when he concluded. Then, as the President and his wife, Florence Kling Harding, left the stand, the Marine Band played "America."

President Harding then revived a custom that had last been followed by Jefferson. He appeared in the Senate Chamber to present, in person, the nominations of the men whom he had selected to be his Cabinet officers.

The First Lady rode with her husband on the return historic trip in

Chief Justice Edward White administers the oath of office to Harding in the new inaugural pavilion, erected at the east portico of the Capitol.

The President, with First Lady Florence Harding, arrives at the White House gate in a Packard Twin Six, following the inauguration at the Capitol. It was the first time that a new President rode to and from the inaugural ceremonies in an automobile.

the Packard Twin Six, but the inaugural parade, in keeping with the President's wishes, consisted of merely a troop of cavalry and a dozen automobiles. Back at the White House the President and First Lady received a delegation of home folks from Marion, Ohio, where the President had been a newspaper editor before becoming a United States Senator from his native state.

There had been controversy over whether or not to have an inaugural ball. In the end the Edward McLeans, friends of the Hardings, gave a private party which the President and First Lady attended that evening.

The simple ceremonies of the day had lacked nothing in impressiveness, and the Harding administration had been launched.

CALVIN COOLIDGE

☆ ☆ ☆

August 3, 1923   March 4, 1925

By the light of a kerosene lamp at 2:47 A.M. on August 3, 1923, Calvin Coolidge took the constitutional oath to become the thirteenth President of the United States. For the first and only time in the history of the nation, a father administered the oath of office to his son when Colonel John C. Coolidge, a notary public and farmer, officiated at the simple ceremony in the tiny New England hamlet of Plymouth Notch, nestled in the Green Mountains of Vermont.

News of the death of President Harding in San Francisco reached Plymouth Notch on the sultry summer night when the husband of the nearest Western Union agent in Bridgewater, eight miles away, arrived at the darkened Coolidge homestead and rapped sharply on the kitchen door to awaken Colonel John. The voice of the 78-year-old man trembled as he called his 51-year-old son, the Vice President, who was sleeping in the room at the top of the stairs. As soon as he had read the official telegram, the younger Coolidge and his wife, Grace, dressed, then knelt down in prayer in which, he later recorded in his autobiography, he asked God to "bless the American people" and give him power to serve them.

A band of newspaper reporters descended on the house and were quickly handed an official statement expressing Coolidge's sympathy and indicating that the following morning he would leave for Washington and take the oath of office there. Hardly had the reporters left when Vermont Congressman Porter Dale arrived with two men. They were L.L. Lane, a railway mail clerk, and Joe Fountain, the editor of the weekly *Springfield Reporter* and stringer for the Associated Press. In

The Coolidge homestead in Plymouth Notch, Vermont. In the first floor room with the bay window, Colonel John Coolidge administered the constitutional oath of office to his son.

persuasive tones, the Congressman was soon imploring Coolidge to take the oath of office immediately because, he stressed, "The country is without a President."

The one telephone in town was located in the general store, whose owner, Florence Cilley, lived in the building and was also the telephone operator. Aroused from her slumber, Miss Cilley put through a call to Washington to Attorney General Harry Daugherty, who gave Coolidge the exact words of the oath which the Vice President's secretary, Edwin Geiser, took down in shorthand. The men walked back to the Coolidge homestead where Geiser made three copies of the oath, each on two-inch wide paper, as Coolidge instructed him.

Then the little group gathered in the front sitting room and as father and son faced each other across the small table, with a shining, pot-bellied kerosene lamp furnishing the only light, Colonel John read the typewritten oath. Phrase by phrase the younger Coolidge, with his right hand raised, repeated the oath. The Bible which had belonged to his mother, who had died when Calvin was twelve years old, lay by his hand, but the President later said it played no official part in the ceremony since it was not the custom to use a Bible in Vermont when an oath was administered. With the final, firm words, "So Help me God," the President took an old steel pen from his father and signed all three copies of the oath. Colonel John signed the oaths, too, and affixed his notary public's seal. On one copy, all of the witnesses signed.

The new President then said "Good night" and turned to follow Mrs. Coolidge up the stairs. Newspaperman Fountain left with his story but Congressman Dale stayed, to travel with the President to Washington later in the day. Railway clerk Lane ensconced himself in the hammock on the front porch, a tiny revolver in his hand. He told later arrivals at the homestead, "I'm guarding Mr. Coolidge. I'm the only Federal official on hand."

As one set of automobile headlights pulled out of the drive, another turned in. Two men from the telephone company in Rutland, twenty-five miles away, arrived to install a telephone for the President at three o'clock in the morning. The President consented and, with Colonel John, watched, intrigued, while Mrs. Coolidge held a kitchen lamp for the men to work by. The phone was ready at three-thirty and all eyes were on the President. He turned the crank, talked to the operator, and was soon put through to Secretary of State Charles Evans Hughes in Washington. He spoke briefly, then hung up the phone, and everyone looked pleased.

At seven o'clock the same morning, the President and Mrs. Coolidge

The kerosene lamp on the table provided the only light for the brief ceremony at 2:47 A.M., August 3, 1923, when Calvin Coolidge took the oath of office.

A smiling Coolidge rides to his inauguration, March 4, 1925, with First Lady Grace Goodhue Coolidge and Kansas Senator Charles Curtis.

The presidential party passes Willard's Hotel on Pennsylvania Avenue on the return trip to the White House after the inauguration.

were dressed and ready for a hearty breakfast in the kitchen before the automobile ride to catch the train for Washington. As soon as his son was on his way, Colonel John made a telephone call. He wanted, he said, the phone taken out at once. And it was.

As the procession of automobiles left the homestead, the Pierce Arrow carrying the President made a detour to the Plymouth Notch cemetery where the President walked up the hill to his mother's grave and, with his wife at his side, stood silently for a few minutes. Then they were driven to Rutland where they boarded a private railroad car, ordered by former Governor Percival Clement, which was hitched onto the "down local," by order of the President.

Less than two years later, on March 4, 1925, Calvin Coolidge took the oath of office in formal inauguration ceremonies at the east portico of the Capitol as the elected President.

The inaugural ceremonies were almost severe in their simplicity by the President's own request, because the Coolidges were officially in mourning for the death of their 16-year-old son, Calvin, Jr. But the rites, strikingly impressive in their unostentatious dignity, marked an historic milestone in the history of inaugurations. For the first time, a former President administered the oath to the President, for William Howard Taft was now Chief Justice of the United States. And for the first time, twenty-five million Americans, tuned in by radio from every part of the nation, simultaneously shared the event with the thousands who thronged the Capitol plaza.

In the Senate Chamber the President witnessed the ceremonies for Vice President Charles G. Dawes. Then he was greeted by "Hail to the Chief" by the Marine Band as he walked to the inaugural stand outside. With little preliminary, Chief Justice Taft recited the oath promptly at one o'clock. Quietly the President murmured: "I do," with his hand resting on the little Bible his mother had given him years before and by which he had learned to read. The President's wife, his father, Colonel John, and his 19-year-old son John were all on the inaugural platform.

In the middle of the President's address, an airplane's motors droned overhead and rumors spread that General Billy Mitchell planned to fly over the crowd and drop posters advocating a unified air service, but the plane disappeared. As the President concluded, he took off his glasses

President Coolidge reviews his inaugural parade from the presidential box in front of the White House on Pennsylvania Avenue.

and grasped the extended hand of Senator Charles Curtis of Kansas. A bugle sounded the signal that the ceremony was over.

The President and Mrs. Coolidge, who was wearing a moonstone gray ensemble, were quickly driven along flag-draped Pennsylvania Avenue, lined with spectators on the beautiful day, back to the White House. There it took less than an hour for the President to review the parade, the last official ceremony of the day.

HERBERT HOOVER

☆ ☆ ☆

March 4, 1929

Herbert Hoover, the first President born west of the Mississippi River, was inaugurated on a rainy Monday, March 4, 1929, in the traditional inaugural pavillion at the east portico of the nation's Capitol.

The 54-year-old Hoover, who had been born in West Branch, Iowa, and as a poor orphan worked his way through Stanford University to become a mining engineer, stood without an overcoat in the chill, with rain spattering his face, during the simple, orderly ceremony that signaled the transfer of executive power from one Republican President to another. The oath was administered at 1:10 P.M. by black-robed Chief Justice Taft, who departed slightly from the text of the Constitution, but not from the meaning, when he pronounced the words "Preserve, maintain and protect" instead of "preserve, protect and defend." A talking newsreel was made during the inauguration—the first of its kind—and the ceremonies were broadcast via networks of radio and short wave to Tokyo, Leningrad, and to Commander Richard E. Byrd's Antarctic camp on a shifting table of polar ice ten thousand miles away.

On the day before the inauguration, Sunday, the President-elect attended services in the Quaker Meeting House, then entertained his chosen Cabinet members at luncheon in his S Street home. Later in the day, with Lou Henry Hoover, his wife, he dined at the White House where President and Mrs. Coolidge also entertained the Vice President-elect Charles Curtis, half Kaw Indian, and his sister, Mrs. Edward Gann. Meanwhile carpenters in front of the White House grounds worked by lantern light to put the finishing touches on the stands along the avenue.

On the inaugural morning, the third cavalry from Fort Myer was

President-elect Herbert Hoover leaves the White House for his inauguration with President Coolidge seated on his right, and accompanied by Senator George Moses, left, front seat, and Representative Bertrand Snell.

massed in Pennsylvania Avenue by the White House to escort President Coolidge and President-elect Hoover, in an open car, to the Capitol. There in the Senate Chamber the two men watched Curtis take the oath, administered to him by the man he succeeded, Vice President Dawes.

The drizzle that started when the presidential party emerged on the platform, which was covered but without sides, had turned into a downpour by the time the new President gave his address in a clear, confident voice before fifty thousand spectators, following the oath. The President's wife and their two sons, Herbert, Jr., with his wife, and young Alan, were in the pavilion. Seated nearby on long wooden benches were several hundred Hooverites who had worked for him in the many relief activities and humanitarian projects he had undertaken during and after the World War.

Following his address, the President turned to his predecessor, whom he had served as Secretary of Commerce, and shook hands with him, which brought enthusiastic shouts from the crowd. Then the former

President and Mrs. Coolidge went directly to the Union Station to take the train for their hometown, Northampton, Massachusetts, while the President and Mrs. Hoover returned to the White House, riding in an open car in the pouring rain. They arrived, drenched, changed to dry clothes, and greeted three hundred luncheon guests before they walked to the enclosed reviewing stand in front of the White House. There, while tens of thousands lined the avenue, waiting patiently in the rain, they watched the most elaborate military and civic parade to celebrate an inauguration in twenty years. Brilliant uniforms turned dull and water-logged, the gay blue and gold decorations—the California colors for the President's state—on the streets drooped, and at the end of the three-hour parade drums no longer drummed, but the President smiled

Universal Cinema Company of Indianapolis, Indiana, incorporated pictures and an excerpt from Hoover's inaugural address in unusual tribute to "our fellow public health workers." In inaugural scene, Chief Justice William H. Taft administers the oath, with First Lady Lou Henry Hoover at left and former President and Mrs. Coolidge at right, behind the new President.

from PRESIDENT HOOVER'S INAUGURAL ADDRESS, MARCH 4, 1929:

"IN public health the discoveries of science have opened a new era. Many sections of our country and many groups of our citizens suffer from diseases the eradication of which are mere matters of administration and moderate expenditure.

"PUBLIC health service should be as fully organized and as universally incorporated in our governmental system as is public education. The returns are a thousand fold in economic benefits and infinitely more in reduction of suffering and promotion of human happiness."

Felicitations to our fellow public health workers.
UNIVERSAL CINEMA COMPANY
Indianapolis, Ind.

Battery C of the Sixteenth Field Artillery in the inaugural parade is reflected in the rain on Pennsylvania Avenue, March 4, 1929.

and waved, applauding picturesque groups that passed by.

One old Confederate veteran proudly marched at the head of the famous Richmond Blues, turning his head smartly to face the President at the command. The distinguished guests in the President's stand rose, waved, some cheered, and the old soldier marched on in the rain. Autos bore the other Civil War veterans in the parade.

Airplanes flew over in formation, barely visible through the clouds but sounding like strident geese. By contrast, the blimp *Los Angeles* sailed serenely low overhead shortly after, followed by one Army and two Navy dirigibles. The President waved at the finale—a group of cowboys who gave the cowboy yell—and returned with Mrs. Hoover and their guests to the White House for a buffet luncheon.

There was no inaugural ball in the official festivities, but a charity inaugural ball that evening in the flag-bedecked Washington Auditorium was formally opened by Vice President Curtis and his sister, Dolly Gann, and included twelve governors among the guests.

FRANKLIN D. ROOSEVELT

☆　☆　☆

March 4, 1933　January 20, 1937

January 20, 1941　January 20, 1945

The only man inaugurated four times as President of the United States was Franklin Delano Roosevelt, whose first inauguration took place during the worst depression in the nation's life and whose last inauguration was in keeping with the austere demands of wartime living, during the critical days of World War II.

Shortly after ten o'clock on Saturday, March 4, 1933, the President-elect and Mrs. Roosevelt, with members of their family, the new Cabinet and their families, arrived at historic St. John's Church on Lafayette Square. There the short prayer service was conducted by the Reverend Endicott Peabody, who had read the marriage vows for Franklin and Eleanor Roosevelt twenty-eight years before, when President Theodore Roosevelt had given the bride away in marriage to her fifth cousin.

Then the Roosevelts were driven in an open limousine around Lafayette Square to the White House, where President Hoover joined the Democratic President-elect for the ride to the Capitol. Mrs. Hoover and Mrs. Roosevelt followed in another limousine, but missing from the cavalcade was Vice President-elect John Nance Garner of Texas, who by-passed "all that formality and tom-foolery stuff," he said, to deliver his farewell address as Speaker of the House. Then he dashed from the House Chamber to the Senate where he was sworn in as Vice President before the two Presidents and a distinguished gathering.

It was bright but chilly on the inaugural platform when Chief Justice Charles Evans Hughes, a former governor of New York, administered the oath to the 50-year-old Roosevelt, another former governor of New York. Roosevelt repeated the oath in its entirety, with his left hand on a seventeenth-century Dutch Bible which had been in his family for nearly 250 years. The passage selected by FDR, on which his hand was placed at each of his four inaugurations, was the thirteenth chapter of the First Epistle of St. Paul to the Corinthians. (The English translation concludes:

". . . and now abideth faith, hope, and love, these three, but the greatest of these is love.")

The President, a gallant figure who could stand only with ten pounds of steel braces around his legs, which had been paralyzed by polio, spoke in clear, ringing accents to the throng of more than 100,000 in the Capitol plaza and to the millions of Americans who listened by radio.

"The only thing we have to fear is fear itself"—the President's confident voice, carried over the crowd by amplifiers, was a rallying cry of hope to a despondent nation. The President's wife, wearing an Eleanor blue velvet dress, and his widowed mother, Sara Delano Roosevelt, watched as the man who had made a comeback from crippling disease outlined a "New Deal" for the economically crippled country.

The capital had discarded its grim forebodings and gave a brilliant celebration for the new President. Flags and bunting gaily decorated the avenue, lined by stands.

Former President Hoover, among the first to congratulate the new President, left the Capitol with Mrs. Hoover to go directly to Union Station where they boarded a train for New York prior to returning to their California home.

Chief Justice Charles Evans Hughes administers the oath to Franklin D. Roosevelt at the Capitol, March 4, 1933. Standing behind the new President, front row, are his son, James, and Herbert Hoover.

Cover sheet of the inaugural program features portraits of Franklin D. Roosevelt and John Nance Garner.

The new President reviewed a long and brilliant inaugural parade, then remained at the White House where he met with Cabinet members and financial experts on the banking crisis, while Mrs. Roosevelt and their children represented him at the inaugural ball held in the Washington Auditorium. After the ball, when the youngest son John, down from Harvard to see his father inaugurated, drove up to the White House gates in his old jalopy in the early hours of the morning, he had a hard time convincing the guard that the White House was, really, his home.

FDR's second inauguration was the first to take place on January 20, under the terms of the Twentieth Amendment to the Constitution, and

Franklin Roosevelt, with First Lady Eleanor Roosevelt at his side, waves a soggy silk hat to crowds lining Pennsylvania Avenue on January 20, 1937, on the return ride from the Capitol to the White House after his second inauguration.

January 20, 1937, was a wet, miserable day. Only the great eagle of the United States, covered by canvas, kept dry at the Capitol. Here for the first time the Vice President, John Garner, was sworn in, for a second term, on the outdoor platform three minutes before a wet, white-whiskered Chief Justice Hughes administered the oath to the President, who repeated it in clarion tones.

As the President addressed an umbrellaed crowd, he paused twice to wipe water from his face. Then he ordered an open limousine and, with Mrs. Roosevelt at his side, rode down the avenue. Early in the day he had said, noticing the people in the streets: "If they can take it, I can," and the people cheered appreciatively as the President and First Lady drove by.

Guests were served luncheon in the East Room while the President stood in an open box—he had ordered the bullet-proof glass removed—

in the reviewing stand, a replica of Jackson's Hermitage, where paper magnolia blossoms melted in the rain, to watch a short parade, only an hour and a half long. Then a tea was held in the East Room and in the evening an inaugural concert, given in Constitution Hall by the National Symphony Orchestra and a Metropolitan Opera quartet, replaced the traditional ball. The President did not attend but was represented by the First Lady.

On January 20, 1941, FDR broke all precedents by becoming the first and only man to be inaugurated President for a third term. The new Vice President, Henry Wallace of Iowa, took his oath of office, administered by retiring Vice President Garner, on the inaugural platform at the Capitol shortly before the President did.

Inauguration day was bright and freezing cold, with a bitter wind, when the Marine Band in new light blue coats announced the President's arrival on the platform with ruffles and flourishes—a salute by drums and bugles—and "Hail to the Chief." For the third time, Chief Justice Hughes administered the oath to the President, who then addressed the people of the United States. The President and First Lady rode in an

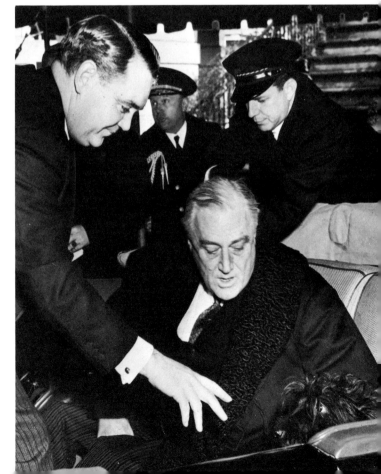

FDR finds a stowaway — his pet scottie, Fala — in his limousine as he leaves the White House for his third inauguration at the Capitol. To Fala's chagrin, he was removed by the President's personal bodyguard, Thomas Qualters (left).

President and Mrs. Roosevelt return to the White House following his third inauguration, January 20, 1941.

Franklin Roosevelt reviews his inaugural parade, January 20, 1941. By the end of the year, the nation was at war.

open car back to the White House where twelve hundred guests, including Norwegian royal refugees Crown Prince Olav and Crown Princess Martha, ate a hearty, cold-weather buffet luncheon in the East Room and State Dining Room before the inaugural parade of predominantly mechanized military. At five o'clock four thousand guests arrived at the White House for tea, and Mrs. Roosevelt and Mrs. Wallace greeted them all. Then the First Lady attended an inaugural concert in Constitution Hall.

Sometime during the day, the President penned a note introducing the defeated Republican candidate, Wendell Willkie, who was leaving soon on a fact-finding trip abroad, to British Prime Minister Winston Churchill. The concluding lines, from a poem by Henry Wadsworth Longfellow, Churchill later wrote, were an inspiration in those perilous times when an invasion attempt of the British Isles by the Nazis was momentarily anticipated:

World War II disabled veterans stand on the south lawn of the White House, alongside ambassadors of foreign nations and members of the United States Congress, to hear Roosevelt's brief, fourth inaugural address.

*The snow-covered White House grounds, shown from the south in this
aerial view, were a winter wonderland of scenic beauty on January 20, 1945,
but for the 7800 guests invited to stand in the slush and drizzle — no umbrellas permitted — it was a cold, wet, miserable day.*

> "Sail on, O Ship of State!
> Sail on, O Union, strong and great!
> Humanity with all its fears,
> With all the hopes for future years,
> Is hanging breathless on thy fate!"

Four years later, the nation was weary after three years of World
War II, and so was President Roosevelt. Over-riding Congressional pro-
tests, the President decided on a "back porch" inauguration for Saturday,
January 20, 1945, and on the south portico of the White House he took
the constitutional oath to begin a fourth term, the only man ever to do so.

The customary pre-inaugural prayer service was held in the East

Room of the White House instead of St. John's, and the inaugural ceremonies, and budget, were cut to the bone. The First Lady, in a sky blue coat and mink scarf, and the widow of President Wilson were among those on the covered south portico. The French windows opened, the Marine Band played "Hail to the Chief," and the President, in a wheelchair pushed by his son James, rolled to the President's platform. Marine Colonel James Roosevelt, who had stood by his father at all four inaugurations, wore a plain Marine field uniform and was the only Roosevelt son present.

There was a brief prayer by the Episcopal Bishop of Washington, Angus Dun, and then the swearing-in ceremony for the new Vice President, Harry S. Truman, took place with the oath administered by retiring Vice President Wallace. The President, wearing a plain business suit, impatiently flung back the Navy cape draped around his shoulders and stood up. He was unable, as usual, to take a single step without aid and he was assisted by his son to the speaker's stand. There, with his hand on the old Dutch Bible, he repeated the constitutional oath after Chief Justice Harlan F. Stone and then delivered a brief address. At the conclusion the Right Reverend John A. Ryan gave the benediction, the blue-clad Marine Band played the national anthem, and the President disappeared within the White House. The solemn and impressive ceremony was over in a few minutes.

A buffet luncheon featuring cold chicken salad—the President had wanted hot chicken à la king—and butterless rolls, in keeping with wartime austerity, was served in the State Dining Room for more than fifteen hundred guests. The ailing President, who had gripped his son's arm in pain after re-entering the White House, later received, with the First Lady, the electors at a reception. Beginning at five o'clock, Mrs. Roosevelt and Mrs. Truman gamely shook hands with an additional thousand guests at tea.

For the Roosevelts, there was a family dinner with their thirteen grandchildren to end the busy inauguration day. There was no parade, no concert, no ball. The harsh realities of war were ever present in the back of everyone's mind.

HARRY S. TRUMAN

☆ ☆ ☆

April 12, 1945   January 20, 1949

On a balmy spring afternoon, Thursday, April 12, 1945, Vice President Harry Truman returned a telephone call from the White House. Steve Early, the President's press secretary, asked the Vice President, then visiting in Speaker of the House Sam Rayburn's office in the Capitol, to come to the White House right away. Without returning to his office, Truman went directly to his car, thus slipping away without even the Secret Service agents assigned to guard him. It was the last time he walked alone through the Capitol. On arriving at the White House he was immediately ushered to Mrs. Roosevelt's study where the First Lady put her arm on his shoulder and said: "Harry, the President is dead."

Thunderstruck by the tragic news, Truman stood speechless, then finally managed to say, "Is there anything I can do for you?" To which Mrs. Roosevelt replied, "Is there anything we can do for you, for you are the one in trouble now."

President Roosevelt had died of a cerebral hemorrhage in Warm Springs, Georgia, that afternoon while Vice President Truman, a little bored as he presided over a windy speech in the Senate, wrote a letter to his mother and sister in Missouri. Less than two hours after arriving at the White House, Truman was sworn into office as President.

The brief, solemn ceremony took place as soon as his wife, Bess Wallace Truman, and their 21-year-old daughter, Margaret, Chief Justice Stone, and members of the Cabinet could be summoned to the White House. There, in the Cabinet room, they assembled to witness the ceremony as the Chief Justice administered the oath, saying "Harry Shippe Truman." The new President answered, "I, Harry S. Truman,"

Crowds gather in Lafayette Square, across Pennsylvania Avenue from the White House, where flag is at half-mast following the death of Franklin Roosevelt that afternoon, April 12, 1945, in Warm Springs, Georgia. Right: Chief Justice Harlan Stone administers the oath to Harry S. Truman at 7:09 P.M. in the White House Cabinet Room, with Mrs. Truman standing between them.

April 12, 1945

Chief Justice Stone officiated as the oath was administered to me in the Cabinet Room under the picture of Woodrow Wilson. I was 7:08 to 7:09 in the afternoon

Harry Truman

I had one h--- scurrying around to find this book on which to take the oath.

Harry Truman's inscription in the 1945 inaugural Bible.

Opposite: On January 20, 1949, Truman, with Vice President Alben Barkley at his side, leads the inaugural parade on Pennsylvania Avenue from the Capitol, flanked by veterans of Battery D, 129th Field Artillery, who served under the command of "Captain Harry" during World War I.

for his middle initial stood for nothing, and had been given to him to please both grandfathers. By a strange coincidence, Truman's great-grandmother was a first cousin of President Tyler, the first Vice President to succeed on the death of a President.

The new President kissed the Bible, and with a sad smile, took the extended hand of the Chief Justice, the first to call him "Mr. President." Then in an emergency meeting the President asked his predecessor's Cabinet to stay on.

The next day the 60-year-old President went back to his old haunt on the Hill, the Capitol, where he had served as Senator from Missouri before being the Senate's presiding officer as Vice President. This time he was not alone, but walked in the center of a square of Secret Servicemen. Before lunch with his old colleagues, he greeted a group of newspaper reporters and shook hands with them, two by two, with tears in his eyes. "If you fellows ever pray," the President said quietly, "please pray for me."

After luncheon as the new President walked through the hall he unexpectedly stepped to the doors of the Senate, threw them open, and silently gazed into the chamber. Then he was gone, with an entourage of Secret Servicemen and a caravan of screaming motorcars trailing after his limousine.

The inauguration on January 20, 1949, was a triumph for the man who had scored the political upset of the century, and the Democrats pulled out all the stops for the celebration which lasted a week. By winning the election over the Republican candidate, Governor Thomas E. Dewey of New York, the incumbent, Harry Truman, had squashed the predictions of the press and the pollsters.

For the President, the inaugural day started with a ham and eggs and hominy grits breakfast with ninety-seven veterans of Battery D, 129th Field Artillery, the guard of honor for their former World War I commander in the inaugural parade. The President insisted that his old buddies still call him "Captain Harry" instead of "Mr. President," and they presented him with a gold-headed ebony cane which the Commander-in-Chief promised to use on his morning walks.

The Trumans and members of the official family attended a pre-inaugural prayer service at St. John's on Lafayette Square, then returned to Blair House, where the first family was living while the White House was being renovated. Then the Joint Committee of Congress arrived to

B-36's of the United States Air Force fly past the Capitol during the inaugural parade, January 20, 1949. Opposite: Fireworks light up the sky in honor of the inauguration of Truman, January 20, 1949. Illuminated Washington Monument is at right, with the Capitol in the distance.

escort the President and Vice President-elect Alben S. Barkley of Kentucky to the Capitol on the brisk, cold, and beautiful day. At a quarter past twelve the two men entered the inaugural stand as the red-coated Marine Band played "Hail to the Chief." The Reverend Edward Hughes Pruden of the First Baptist Church said the invocation, Phil Regan sang the national anthem, and Supreme Court Associate Justice Stanley Reed administered the oath to Vice President Barkley.

For the second time, Harry S. Truman took the short constitutional oath prescribed for the President, this time before more than 100,000 spectators who filled the Capitol plaza and overflowed. Television, for the first time, carried the dramatic inaugural spectacle simultaneously to millions of viewers. The President's left hand rested on two Bibles, the one on which he had taken the oath three years and nine months before, and a facsimile of the Gutenberg Bible presented to him by the citizens of his hometown, Independence, Missouri. Chief Justice Fred Vinson administered the oath, the President repeated it and kissed the Bible, then shook hands with both the Chief Justice and the new Vice President before delivering a forceful address.

After a quick luncheon in the Capitol, in the office of the Senate secretary Leslie Biffle, the President revived an old tradition by leading the inaugural parade himself under dazzling skies down Pennsylvania Avenue, lined with one million people who shared the excitement of the

gay parade—a striking contrast to the military might of the 1941 parade. A motorcycle escort, forming the initials "H T," preceded the President, and an armada of airplanes zoomed overhead as the procession neared the White House reviewing stand, from which the President and Vice President watched the seven-mile-long parade that included a mule-drawn float from Lamar, Missouri—the President's birthplace—and an old fashioned calliope, tooting "I'm Just Wild About Harry," that brought up the rear. Late in the afternoon President and Mrs. Truman held a reception for grass roots Democratic campaign workers at the National Gallery of Art.

The big day ended with an inaugural ball at the National Guard Armory, jammed by nearly ten thousand persons. The happy President, wearing white tie and tails, shook hands with hundreds who made their way to the Presidential box in the balcony. The First Lady, dressed in black velvet trimmed with Alençon lace, watched with him as their daughter Margaret whirled on the dance floor and Benny Goodman, Guy Lombardo, and Xavier Cugat and their bands played. Thousands of American roses, Colorado carnations, and gardenias from Mexico transformed the gym-like Armory into a flower garden.

It was after one-thirty when a beaming President Truman waved and smiled a good-bye to the celebrating throng. It had been, he said, "a gorgeous day, in every sense of the word."

DWIGHT D. EISENHOWER

☆ ☆ ☆

January 20, 1953   January 20 & 21, 1957

General of the Army Dwight David Eisenhower, the most popular hero of World War II, became President on January 20, 1953, after winning the votes of the American people with the ease that his famous smile had won the affection of kings and commoners the world around. Known to all as "Ike," the 62-year-old West Point graduate was the first professional soldier since General Grant to become President, and the first Republican to be inaugurated in twenty-four years. There were three days of victorious celebrations, but the President-elect announced that he would attend only the inaugural ceremonies and the ball, and wear a homburg instead of a formal high silk hat. He reminded friends who complained about his choice of headgear that Presidents would still be wearing knee breeches and cocked hats if tradition were always followed.

For the first time in twenty years a retiring President and President-elect rode side by side down Pennsylvania Avenue as President Truman and General Eisenhower led the four-car caravan from the White House to the Capitol. There the sun broke through the misty morning to shine brightly on the inaugural drama on the presidential platform, where at 12:32 P.M. Dwight David Eisenhower repeated the oath after Chief Justice Vinson.

President Truman had ordered General Eisenhower's only son, John, a West Point officer, brought back from the Korean War to the United States to attend his father's inauguration. General Eisenhower's four brothers and former President Hoover were also on the inaugural platform. The program opened with singing by the red-robed Defiance

President Truman and President-elect Dwight D. Eisenhower exchange greetings at the White House prior to riding to the Capitol for the inaugural ceremonies. From left are Margaret Truman, Mrs. Eisenhower, Mrs. Truman.

College choir from Ohio, followed by the national anthem sung by soprano Dorothy Maynor, and tenor Eugene Conly's rendition of "America the Beautiful." Prayers by two religious leaders were offered, and Richard M. Nixon was sworn in as Vice President before the ceremonies for the new President.

General Eisenhower took the oath with his left hand resting on two Bibles—the small, black-bound West Point Bible which his mother had given him when he graduated from the Military Academy in 1915, and the eighteenth-century Bible on which George Washington had taken the oath as the first President. Eisenhower grinned happily and shook hands with Chief Justice Vinson as the crowd cheered; then walked over to his wife, Mamie Doud Eisenhower, and kissed her. After putting on his glasses, the President departed from the prepared text of his inaugural address to offer "a little prayer of my own," as he said. That morning, after returning from a pre-inaugural service at the National Presbyterian Church to his suite at the Statler-Hilton Hotel, he had asked his wife, "Mamie, what do you think of my saying a prayer?" Encouraged by her, he promptly wrote down his thoughts and composed the first President's prayer for his own inauguration.

The new President lunched in the Capitol before leading the grand parade, which included 62 bands and 26,000 participants, down the avenue. Former President Truman and his family were guests at a luncheon in the Dean Acheson home before leaving by train for Mis-

General Eisenhower responds to the crowds along Pennsylvania Avenue as he rides in the inaugural parade from the Capitol to the White House, January 20, 1953.

The colors of the West Point cadets salute as they arrive at the President's reviewing stand in front of the White House during the inauguration parade, January 20, 1953. Warm memories of the parade of 1913, when young Cadet Eisenhower from Abilene, Kansas, had marched smartly by President Wilson, came to Eisenhower's mind as the cadets swung by.

Chief Justice Earl Warren officiates at the private swearing-in ceremony for Eisenhower at the White House, Sunday, January 20, 1957.

Contralto Marian Anderson sings "The Star Spangled Banner" at the public inauguration for President Eisenhower (left of Miss Anderson) and Vice President Richard Nixon (right), held at the Capitol Monday, January 21, 1957.

souri. Despite the President's request that the parade be short and simple —he had vetoed fireworks for the evening—the Republicans wanted to celebrate and it was almost seven o'clock before the last elephant passed by the President's stand.

A few hours later the beaming President and First Lady arrived, to ruffles and flourishes and "Hail to the Chief," at the brilliant inaugural ball sites, first at the National Guard Armory and then at Georgetown University's McDonough Hall. Six orchestras played for dancing at the two balls, which were packed to the doors, but most people preferred to stand and stare at the new President and at the First Lady, whose pink peau de soie gown embroidered with beads glittered in the brilliant spotlight. At last, in the early morning hours of January 21, President and Mrs. Eisenhower returned to their new home—the White House.

For Eisenhower's second inauguration, there was another big spectacle, parade, and smashing ball on Monday, January 21, 1957, but the official ceremony had first taken place quietly on Sunday, January 20, in the White House, when Chief Justice Earl Warren administered the constitutional oath to the President. No newspaper reporters were allowed at the private ceremony, held about 10:28 A.M. after the President with Mrs. Eisenhower and his official family had attended church services conducted by the Reverend Edward Elson at National Presby-

President Eisenhower with his grandchildren, Barbara and Dwight David Eisenhower II, watch the inaugural parade, January 21, 1957, from the presidential reviewing stand with Vice President Nixon and his daughters, Julie and Tricia (right). Even then it would seem that David only had eyes for Julie.

President and Mrs. Eisenhower, with their son and daughter-in-law, Major and Mrs. John Eisenhower, greet crowds at the inaugural ball, January 21, 1957. First Lady Mamie Doud Eisenhower chose a citron yellow gown, sparkling with brilliants, for the celebration.

terian Church. The President's West Point Bible was opened to the Thirty-third Psalm when he repeated the oath both on Sunday morning and again on Monday at the Capitol ceremony. Vice President Nixon was also sworn in for a second time at both ceremonies.

At the Capitol, Marian Anderson sang "The Star Spangled Banner," two clergymen offered prayers, and the short, dignified ceremony was seen by more Americans than ever before in history, for there were nearly sixty million television sets in the nation, compared to twenty-one million only four years before. Following the President's short inaugural address, the old soldier President was cheered by more than 200,000 who lined the avenue. That evening the President and First Lady beamed and waved at the celebrating crowds at all four inaugural ball sites, before Ike, the first President limited to two terms under the Twenty-second Amendment, got down to business for another four years.

JOHN F. KENNEDY

☆　☆　☆

January 20, 1961

John Fitzgerald Kennedy, the first President born in the twentieth century, told the world in tones as clear and crisp as his inaugural day: "Let the word go forth from this time and place, to friend and foe alike, that the torch has been passed to a new generation of Americans —born in this century, tempered by war, disciplined by a hard and bitter peace, proud of our ancient heritage . . ."

It was January 20, 1961, and the youngest man, at forty-three, ever elected to the Presidency had just taken the constitutional oath of office, administered by Chief Justice Warren, on a Rheims-Douay version of the Bible, an authorized translation of the Roman Catholic Church, for John Kennedy was also the first Roman Catholic to become President of the United States. Ten minutes before, Vice President Lyndon B. Johnson had been sworn into office by Speaker of the House Sam Rayburn.

A raging snowstorm that had started the day before had dumped six inches of fresh snow, turning the capital into chaos, but three thousand servicemen with seven hundred trucks, snowplows, and army flame throwers had worked all night to clear the way from the White House to the Capitol before the two top-hatted Presidents rode in a bubbletop limousine up the historic avenue for the noon ceremonies. Kennedy began his inauguration day by attending nine o'clock Mass at Holy Trinity Roman Catholic Church, which was decorated with red, white, and blue carnations. About eleven o'clock, with Jacqueline Bouvier Kennedy, his wife, and his Congressional escort he was driven to the White House where President Eisenhower had altered the official

President Eisenhower and President-elect John F. Kennedy leave the White House for the inauguration at the Capitol, January 20, 1961.

Crowds at the Capitol for the inauguration of Kennedy. Inaugural platform is at left.

John Kennedy, with hand raised, takes the oath of office, administered by Chief Justice Warren, on the inaugural platform at the Capitol.

schedule by inviting the Kennedys to come early for coffee on the icy morning.

In the brilliant aftermath of the storm, the newly renovated and expanded east portico of the Capitol, and the dome looming overhead, gleamed against the clear blue sky, a beautiful background for the inaugural drama that unfolded on the Presidential platform. There, at the President's request, contralto Marian Anderson again sang "The Star Spangled Banner," and the octogenarian New England poet Robert Frost rose to read a poem he had written for the occasion. Blinded in the bright glare of the snow, the venerable white-haired poet stumbled over his own words and Vice President-elect Johnson stepped forward to shade the page with his top hat. Frost, undaunted, skipped the new dedication and recited from memory his older poem, "The Gift Outright..."

A Kennedy family friend, Richard Cardinal Cushing of Boston, gave the invocation, the first of several prayers offered by leaders of different faiths, and for several agonizing minutes it looked as though the wooden inaugural stand might go up in smoke. Wisps curled up from the lectern while the unperturbed prelate prayed on, with Secret Servicemen and firemen crawling on the red carpet to find the cause—a short circuit.

President Kennedy delivers his address before a battery of newspaper and television cameras and a crowd of thousands in the east Capitol park.

First Lady Jacqueline Bouvier Kennedy, wearing a mink-trimmed beige costume, accompanies her husband as he leads the inaugural parade on the return to the White House.

President Kennedy, with Vice President Johnson at his side, reviews his inaugural parade from the presidential stand in front of the White House.

While spectators in the Capitol plaza pulled blankets around them to keep warm, President Kennedy took off his overcoat and stood bareheaded during the ceremonies. In the 22-degree chill and bitter wind, he delivered his address, with puffs of white steam punctuating the air as he spoke. Former President Truman and his wife were on the platform in the bright, freezing cold, but former President Hoover, also invited, had circled a Washington airport in a plane unable to land the night before. The ceremonies over, President Kennedy had a lobster luncheon in the old Supreme Court Chamber in the Capitol. Former President Eisenhower went off to lunch with friends at the 1925 F Street Club, traded his topper for a familiar homburg, and, with Mrs. Eisenhower, was driven eighty-five miles to his Gettysburg, Pennsylvania, farm that afternoon.

The President, with Mrs. Kennedy wearing a mink-trimmed beige costume by his side, rode down the avenue in an open car to lead his inaugural parade. His parents, former Ambassador and Mrs. Joseph Kennedy, arrived at the reviewing stand before the President did and as the President's limousine pulled up, father and son stood to salute each other. For the President, the high point of the parade was a float bearing the last World War II PT boat, painted "PT 109" as a facsimile of the craft which he had commanded as a young Navy lieutenant. The President waved and called out "Great Work!" as the surviving crew members of his old PT 109, standing on the boat, saluted the Commander-in-Chief as they went by.

After the three-hour parade, a private dinner for the President was given in the home of an old schoolmate, George Wheeler II. It was followed by a quick visit to a dinner that singer Frank Sinatra was giving for the entertainers at the Inaugural Gala, which the President-elect and his wife had attended the evening before.

For the first time the inaugural ball was distributed over five ball sites, and the President made the rounds of them all. The First Lady smiled happily at her husband's side at the National Guard Armory and the Mayflower Hotel balls, but then returned to the White House. She was recovering from the Caesarean birth of their son, John, Jr., only eight weeks before.

The President was the despair of the Secret Servicemen, who tried to keep up with him in the crowded ballrooms. Climbing over chairs

In the only PT boat extant, representing PT 109 which was cut in two by a Japanese destroyer during World War II, surviving crew members salute their old commander as they pass the presidential reviewing stand.

when there was no other way to get there, the President hopped around to surrounding boxes to greet friends. When former President and Mrs. Truman were escorted to Kennedy's Mayflower box, both the new President and the crowd stood to appaud the elder statesman and his wife. At one ball, waiters wore gloves and male guests wore long underwear beneath their white ties and tails while the ladies shivered in fashionable finery. At another, the President gaily said: "I'm here tonight representing my wife. This is an ideal place to spend the evening and I hope we can meet here again tomorrow at one o'clock and do it all over again."

After the fifth ball JFK stepped into his limousine and sped off for a nightcap at the Georgetown home of columnist Joseph Alsop, emerging several hours later puffing a long cigar. Then the new President spent his first night in the White House sleeping in the historic Lincoln bed. It was the beginning of his ill-fated term of a thousand days which was to end for Kennedy as Lincoln's stay in the White House had—on a catafalque in the East Room.

LYNDON B. JOHNSON

☆ ☆ ☆

November 22, 1963   January 20, 1965

On November 22, 1963, the thirty-sixth President of the United States took the constitutional oath of office in the cabin of the President's airplane, *Air Force One*, Aircraft 26000, in the immediate shocking moment of national tragedy. Vice President Lyndon Baines Johnson had succeeded to the Presidency on the assassination of John Kennedy, shot down as he rode in a motorcade through the streets of Dallas, Texas.

Johnson was whisked from Parkland Hospital, where President Kennedy lay dead, to the presidential plane which stood on the runway of Love Field on the outskirts of Dallas. There, while a secretary took down the words of the oath, repeated on the telephone by Deputy Attorney General Nicholas Katzenbach in Washington, Air Force One waited for Mrs. Kennedy and the casket carrying the body of the slain President. Federal Judge Sarah T. Hughes of the Northern District of Texas—a Kennedy appointee—arrived, at Johnson's request, to administer the oath of office.

It was 2:39 P.M. Central Standard Time—less than two hours after President Kennedy's death—when President Johnson repeated the oath with his left hand on a small, soft, leather-bound Catholic missal that had been found in the President's bedroom on the plane. As Judge Hughes became the first woman to administer the oath to the President, tears came to her eyes and her voice faltered. On the new President's right stood his wife and on his left, Mrs. Kennedy, her pink suit caked with her husband's blood. The President's voice was almost inaudible as he repeated the oath. Then he turned to kiss Mrs. Johnson and Mrs. Kennedy each gently on the cheek. The grief-stricken group that had

187

gathered in the stateroom moved about the plane as if in a walking nightmare, and Lady Bird Johnson took Jacqueline Kennedy's hand. "The whole nation mourns your husband," she said quietly.

As White House photographer Captain Cecil Stoughton, who had recorded the brief ceremony, and Judge Hughes left the plane, the President gave the order to take off. Little more than two hours later the giant jet landed at Andrews Air Force Base in Washington. President and Mrs. Johnson waited quietly while the Kennedy aides escorted the slain President's casket down the ramp, leaving the new President and his wife behind alone. A short time later they stepped from the plane into the spotlight by the waiting microphones where the tall, 55-year-old, Texas-born President said a few words, concluding, "I will do my best. That is all I can do. I ask for your help—and God's." Then the Johnsons walked to a waiting helicopter which took them to the White House grounds, and while Mrs. Johnson went to their northwest Washington home, The Elms, the new President went to his old office in the Executive Office Building. There, sometime during that evening, he penned two private notes to the late President's children, six-year-old Caroline and John, Jr., whose third birthday was to fall on the day of his father's funeral. Later, in the early morning hours of November 23, the new President was escorted to his home by Secret Servicemen with drawn sidearms. The transition of power had taken place, but the new President and the nation were stunned by tragedy.

When Lyndon Baines Johnson was inaugurated on January 20, 1965, he had won a four-year term in the White House by the greatest margin of the popular vote—15,000,000—in the nation's history. "It's a great and wonderful day," the President murmured, shortly after delivering his inaugural address at the Capitol where the portable canopied platform had been erected for the traditional ceremonies. But there were sad reminders of the vulnerability of Presidents, for Johnson rode in a bullet-proof, closed limousine and stood behind bullet-proof glass in an armored reviewing stand to watch his inaugural parade.

It was Lyndon Johnson's day, and he put his own special brand on every phase of the festivities, from the moment he attended the inaugural concert in Constitution Hall to hear young Texas pianist Van Cliburn play on the eve of the inauguration until he left the last of five inaugural balls, a few minutes past midnight the following night.

With his personal and official families, the President had attended

Lyndon Baines Johnson takes the oath of office, administered by Federal Judge Sarah T. Hughes (back to camera) in the stateroom of the Presidential jet, Air Force One, at Love Field, Dallas, Texas, on November 22, 1963. At the new President's right stands his wife and at his left, Mrs. John F. Kennedy, widow of the assassinated President.

Aboard Air Force One, the Presidential Aircraft Boeing VC-137C, here pictured in flight, Lyndon B. Johnson took the oath of office as President of the United States on November 22, 1963, following the assassination of John F. Kennedy.

Mrs. Lyndon Johnson holds the family Bible while Chief Justice Warren administers the oath of office to Johnson (left, center) in the inaugural ceremonies at the Capitol, January 20, 1965.

The President and First Lady, left, with Vice President and Mrs. Hubert Humphrey, watch the colorful parade from the reviewing stand in front of the White House.

National City Christian Church, with leaders of several religions participating in the special services, to start the bright, cold inauguration day. Wide-brimmed Stetsons abounded in Washington checkrooms and Texas cowboy boots walked the streets of the Nation's capital, and the President reverted to homespun simplicity by wearing a plain, oxford gray business suit instead of formal morning clothes for his inaugural ceremonies. Later, black tie was the order of the President at the inaugural ball.

As the President stood before Chief Justice Warren to repeat the oath he had taken fourteen months before, Mrs. Johnson stepped forward to hold the family Bible, a gift of the President's late mother, Rebekah Baines Johnson. It was the first time that a President's wife had taken a role in the inaugural ceremony and the First Lady, wearing an American Beauty red coat and hat, shared the solemn and dignified moment with obvious pride in her husband as their two college-age daughters, Lynda and Luci, watched. Shortly before, Vice President Hubert Humphrey had been sworn into office by Speaker of the House John McCormack. At the ceremonies, Metropolitan Opera soprano Leontyne Price sang "America the Beautiful," the President's own Marine Band played, and, at the President's request, the Mormon Tabernacle choir sang "This Is

The Old Guard Fife and Drum Corps passing the presidential reviewing stand during the inaugural parade.

President and Mrs. Johnson and Vice President and Mrs. Humphrey arrive in the Presidential box at the National Guard Armory inaugural ball. The First Lady, waving to the ballgoers, wore a jonquil yellow satin gown with matching sable-cuffed coat.

My Country." There were prayers offered by various religious leaders before the simple oath-taking and the short, softly spoken address.

After lunch in the old Supreme Court Chamber, the President started on his way down the avenue where he spotted the band of his alma mater, Southwest Texas State College, waiting to lead the marching units in the inaugural parade. At the corner of Third Street and Constitution Avenue, the President leaped out of his bullet-proof limousine to greet the contingent of young people from the college he had worked his way through many years before.

There were five inaugural ball sites and the President, with the First Lady, wearing a "Yellow Rose of Texas" gown especially designed for her, and their daughters, stopped by them all. To the delight of the ballgoers and the dismay of the Secret Service, the President led out the dancing with his wife at one ball, and at another swooped Margaret Truman Daniel over the railing of her box onto the dance floor. Mrs. Daniel was the personal representative of her father, former President Truman, for the inauguration. Twenty-eight thousand people had paid $25 each to attend the ball and, as the President quipped: "Never before have so many paid so much to dance so little!"

RICHARD M. NIXON

☆ ☆ ☆

January 20, 1969

Richard Milhous Nixon, who made the most spectacular political comeback of the century to become President of the United States, was inaugurated on Monday, January 20, 1969. The 56-year-old Republican President had served in the Congress and then as Vice President in the administration of President Eisenhower, but was defeated by John Kennedy in the 1960 election. As Nixon, the first man born west of the Rockies to be elected President, took the oath of office his hand rested on two family, nineteenth-century Bibles, held by his wife, Patricia Ryan Nixon, opened to Isaiah 11, 4: "And he shall judge among the nations, and shall rebuke many people; and they shall beat their swords into plowshares, and their spears into pruning hooks: nation shall not lift up sword against nation, neither shall they learn war any more."

Chief Justice Warren administered the oath, shook hands, and congratulated the new President who then stood erectly, with Mrs. Nixon at his side, while the Marine Band greeted him with "Hail to the Chief." As the 21-gun salute rang out on the Capitol grounds, the President escorted the new First Lady to her seat before delivering a low-keyed inaugural address in a calm, confident voice. The day threatened rain and snow, but the sun peered through gray clouds on the inaugural drama in the traditional Corinthian-columned pavilion, this day sheltered by bullet-proof glass.

As crowds jammed the Capitol grounds, countless millions heard by radio and watched by television, for the short, solemn ceremony that transferred the power and the burden of the Presidency to California-born Richard Nixon, a man of Quaker heritage, was relayed by satellite

Chief Justice Warren is the first to congratulate President Richard Nixon after administering the oath of office while First Lady Patricia Nixon, holding the two family Bibles used in the ceremony, beams her approval. Applauding are former President Johnson, left, Vice President Spiro Agnew, and former Vice President Humphrey.

Field guns are fired in salute to Nixon following the inaugural ceremony at the Capitol, January 20, 1969.

around the world. Minutes before Spiro T. Agnew had taken the oath as Vice President.

When Nixon spoke the simple, 35-word oath, linking him like a chain to that first inauguration almost 180 years before, it was the climax of three days of festivities. On the platform were the President and Mrs. Nixon's two daughters, 22-year-old Tricia, and 20-year-old Julie with her young husband, the grandson and namesake of former President Dwight David Eisenhower. General Eisenhower lay ill in Walter Reed Hospital where he watched the inauguration on television while being well represented by his family at the ceremonies.

For the President-elect, the round of celebrations had started the day before when he flew from New York to Washington in time to attend the inaugural concert at Constitution Hall with Mrs. Nixon. On the inaugural morning, the President, with Mrs. Nixon who was wearing a cyclamen pink wool coat with sable hat and tie, entered a bubble-top presidential limousine at the Statler-Hilton Hotel. They were driven to the State Department for a 9:30 A.M. interfaith prayer breakfast. After returning to their hotel the Nixons, with their daughters and son-in-law, went on to the White House where they were greeted by President and Mrs. Johnson and their daughters—now Lynda Robb and Luci Nugent. In the White House Red Room the President and First Lady entertained at an informal coffee for the Nixons with the outgoing Vice President and Mrs. Humphrey, and the Vice President-elect and Mrs. Agnew, and their family, also as guests.

Then the two Presidents led the procession in a closed limousine from the White House to the Capitol for the ceremonies, which included a series of prayers by representatives of several faiths, music by the Marine Band and the Mormon Tabernacle choir. After the ceremonies on the platform, the new President with his family was honored at luncheon in the Capitol. Former President Johnson and his family had luncheon in the suburban Maryland home of his former Secretary of Defense, Clark Clifford, and then flew back to their Texas home on *Air Force One*, the same plane on which Johnson had taken the oath of office and traveled from Texas to Washington on that black November 22, 1963.

As the new President and First Lady led the inaugural parade down Pennsylvania Avenue, the tightest security measures were in effect. Windows on all buildings along the parade route were closed and entrance to the buildings was by authorized permit only. Soldiers lined the street and confetti and streamers were prohibited, but Boy Scouts

President and Mrs. Nixon, with the bubble-top of the presidential limousine open, respond to crowds along Pennsylvania Avenue near the White House on the return from the Capitol inaugural ceremonies.

Nixon applauds his inaugural parade from the reviewing stand with Mrs. Nixon and Mrs. Dwight D. Eisenhower (front row), and Tricia Nixon, Julie Nixon Eisenhower and her husband, David, in the second row behind the President. Mr. and Mrs. John Eisenhower are in the third row.

The Nixon inaugural theme float, "Forward Together," turns from Pennsylvania Avenue into Fifteenth Street during the inaugural parade.

passed out small American flags for spectators to wave.

The President and first family watched the parade for almost three hours. As the high-stepping marchers went by the presidential box, none received bigger smiles and applause than the band from Whittier High School, where Dick Nixon had been an outstanding debater. Colorado sent a ski jump on its float, and there were the handsome Culver Black Horse Cavalry cadets, popular as always. Then the President and Mrs. Nixon went back to the White House and mingled with 150 relatives at a private, informal reception where hot tea and coffee and both hot and cold hors d'oeuvres, but no alcoholic beverages, were served.

It was raining in the evening, but the President and First Lady did the town, taking in all six inaugural ball sites where the President greeted thirty-thousand dancers who had paid $35.00 apiece to celebrate his inauguration. In addition to the ballrooms of five hotels, the handsome white marble Smithsonian Museum of History and Technology was the scene of an inaugural ball, where Duke Ellington's band—a favorite

Standing in front of the original Star Spangled Banner, which inspired Francis Scott Key to write the words of the national anthem during the War of 1812, Nixon greets inaugural ballgoers in the Smithsonian Institution's Museum of History and Technology. The First Lady wears a mimosa yellow satin gown and jacket encrusted with shimmering Austrian crystal jewels, and embroidered with Byzantine scrolls of gold and silver bullion.

of the new President—was one of those playing during the gala evening. Guests danced around locomotives, covered wagons, a water wheel, and under the watchful eye of the statue of Washington which in years past had witnessed inaugurations from the Capitol steps. Before the Star Spangled Banner which had been visible by the "rockets' red glare'" as it flew over Fort McHenry the night of September 13, 1814, the President faced one of the biggest throngs of the evening.

"In the years ahead," he said, "we will look back on this night. We will forget it was cold today and rained tonight, but we will remember the warm glow of this evening and the warmth of your friendship."

BIBLIOGRAPHY

☆ ☆ ☆

Abbott, John S. C., and Russell H. Conwell. *Lives of the Presidents of the United States*. Portland, Maine: H. Hallett & Co., 1882.

Abell, Alexander G. *Life of John Tyler*. New York: Harper & Bros., 1843.

Abraham Lincoln From His Own Words and Contemporary Accounts. Edited by Roy Edgar Appleman. Washington, D.C.: National Park Service, 1942 (Reprint 1961).

Adams, Abigail. *Letters of Mrs. Adams, the Wife of John Adams, with an introductory memoir by her grandson, Charles Francis Adams*. Second Ed. 2 vols. Boston: Charles C. Little and James Brown, 1840.

Adams, John. *The Works of John Adams with Life, Introduction and Illustrations by his grandson Charles Francis Adams*. Boston: Little, Brown & Company, 1854.

Adams, John Quincy. *Memoirs of John Quincy Adams, comprising portions of His Diary from 1795 to 1848*. Edited by Charles Francis Adams. Philadelphia: J. B. Lippincott & Co., 1874-77.

Adams Papers, microfilm edition. Quotations from the diaries and letters of John Adams, Abigail Adams, and John Quincy Adams from the *Adams Papers* are from the microfilm edition, and are reprinted by permission of the Massachusetts Historical Society.

Aikman, Lonnelle. *The Living White House*. Washington, D.C.: White House Historical Association with the cooperation of the National Geographic Society Special Publications Division, 1966.

Aikman, Lonnelle. *We, the People. The Story of the United States Capitol*. Washington, D.C.: The United States Capitol Historical Society in cooperation with the National Geographic Society, 1969.

American Gallery of Portraits of the Presidents, The. Pub. by Guy Galterman, St. Louis, Mo., 1958.

American Heritage Pictorial History of the Presidents of the United States, The. Editor in charge Kenneth W. Leish (by the editors of American Heritage, The Magazine of History). 2 vols. New York: American Heritage Publishing Co., Inc., 1968.

Ames, Mary Clemmer. *Ten Years in Washington. Life and Scenes in the Na-*

tional Capital, as a Woman Sees Them. Hartford, Conn.: A. D. Worthington & Co., Publishers, 1875.

Annual Report of the American Historical Association for the Year 1913. Vol. II. *Papers of James A. Bayard 1796-1815.* Edited by Elizabeth Donnan. Washington, 1913.

Baldridge, Letitia. *Of Diamonds and Diplomats.* Boston: Houghton Mifflin Company, 1968.

Barre, W. L. *The Life and Public Services of Millard Fillmore.* Buffalo: Wanzer, McKim & Co., 1856.

Baughman, U. E. *Secret Service Chief.* New York: Harper & Bros., 1961.

Bishop, Jim. *The Day Kennedy Was Shot.* New York: Funk & Wagnalls, 1968.

Bobbé, Dorothie. *Mr. and Mrs. John Quincy Adams.* New York: Minton, Balch & Company, 1930.

Bowen, Catherine Drinker. *Biography: The Craft and The Calling.* Boston, Toronto: Little, Brown and Company, 1969.

Bowen, Catherine Drinker. *Miracle at Philadelphia.* Boston: Little, Brown and Company, 1966.

Briggs, Emily Edson. *The Olivia Letters.* New York and Washington: The Neale Publishing Company, 1906.

Brown, Margaret W. *The Dresses of the First Ladies of the White House.* Washington: Smithsonian Institution, 1952.

Bryan, Wilhelmus Bogart. *A History of the National Capital.* 2 vols. New York: The Macmillan Co., 1914.

Buel, Julia Maria. *Inauguration Day, March 4, 1861.* Detroit: Friends of the Detroit Public Library, Inc., 1960.

Busey, Samuel C. "The Centennial of the First Inauguration of a President at the Permanent Seat of the Government." *Records of the Columbia Historical Society,* Vol. 5. Washington: Columbia Historical Society, 1901.

Cable, Mary. *The Avenue of the Presidents.* Boston: Houghton, Mifflin Company, 1969.

Carpenter, Frank G. *Carp's Washington.* Edited by Frances Carpenter. New York, Toronto, London: McGraw-Hill Company, Inc., 1960.

Chalmers. John P. *Presidential Inaugural Bibles: An Exhibition.* Washington: The Rare Book Library, Washington Cathedral, 1968.

Chamberlain, I. *Biography of Millard Fillmore.* Buffalo: Thomas & Lathrops, 1856.

Churchill, Winston S. *The Grand Alliance.* Boston: Houghton, Mifflin Company, 1950.

Clark, Allen C. "Abraham Lincoln in the National Capital." *Records of the Columbia Historical Society,* Vol. 27. Washington: Columbia Historical Society, 1925.

Colman, Edna M. *Seventy-Five Years of White House Gossip.* Garden City, New York: Doubleday, Page & Company, 1926.

Colman, Edna M. *White House Gossip, from Andrew Johnson to Calvin Coolidge.* Garden City, N.Y.: Doubleday, Page & Company, 1927.

Columbia Historical Society. *Records of the Columbia Historical Society*, Washington.

Coolidge, Calvin. *The Autobiography of Calvin Coolidge*. New York: Cosmopolitan Book Corporation, 1929.

Crook, William H. *Memories of the White House*. Compiled and edited by Henry Rood. Boston: Little, Brown and Company, 1911.

Devens, R. M. *Great Events of the Past Century*. 1878.

Dickens, Charles. *American Notes*. London: Chapman & Hall, 1913.

Drury, Allen. *A Senate Journal (1943-1945)*. New York, Toronto, London: McGraw-Hill Book Company, Inc., 1963.

Durant, John and Alice. *Pictorial History of American Presidents*. New York: A. S. Barnes and Company, 1955.

Eisenhower, Dwight D. *The White House Years: Mandate for Change*. Garden City, New York: Doubleday and Co., 1963.

Ellet, Elizabeth F. L. *The Queens of American Society*. Philadelphia: Porter & Coates, 1867.

Fay, Paul B., Jr., *The Pleasure of His Company*. New York: Harper & Row, Publishers, Inc., 1966.

Fountain, Joe H. *Homestead Inaugural*. St. Albans, Vermont, 1950.

Franklin Pierce of New Hampshire Becomes 14th President of the United States. Published for the State of New Hampshire, Recreation Division, by The Lloyd Hills Press: Bethlehem, N.H.

Freidel, Frank. *The Presidents of the United States of America*. Washington, D.C.: White House Historical Association, 1964.

Furman, Bess. *White House Profile*. Indianapolis & New York: The Bobbs-Merrill Company, Inc., 1951.

Graff, Robert D., Robert Emmett Ginna, and Roger Butterfield. *FDR*. New York, Evanston, London: Harper & Row, Publishers, 1963.

Green, Constance McLaughlin. *Washington, Capital City, 1879-1950*. Princeton, New Jersey: Princeton University Press, 1963.

Green, Constance McLaughlin. *Washington, Village and Capital, 1800-1878*. Princeton, New Jersey: Princeton University Press, 1962.

Hillman, William. *Mr. President*. New York: Farrar, Straus and Young, 1952.

Holloway, Laura C. *The Ladies of the White House; or, In the Home of the Presidents*. Philadelphia: Bradley & Company, 1881.

Hoover, Irwin Hood (Ike). *Forty-Two Years in the White House*. Boston and New York: Houghton Mifflin Company, 1934.

Horan, James D. *Matthew Brady: Historian with a Camera*. New York: Crown Publishers, 1955.

Hurd, Charles. *The White House Story*. New York: Hawthorn Books, Inc., Publishers, 1966.

Hurja, Emil Edward. *History of Presidential Inaugurations*. New York: New York Democrat Pub. Corp., 1933.

Hutchins, Stilson and Joseph W. Moore. *The National Capital*. Washington: Post Pub. Co., 1885.

BIBLIOGRAPHY

Inaugural Addresses of the Presidents of the United States. Washington, D.C.: United States Government Printing Office, 1969.

Inaugural Story, The. Created and Produced by The American Heritage Magazine and the 1969 Inaugural Book Committee. New York: American Heritage Publishing Co., Inc., 1969.

Irving, Washington. *Life of George Washington.* New York: G. P. Putnam, 1855-59.

James, Marquis. *Andrew Jackson: Portrait of a President.* Indianapolis & New York: The Bobbs-Merrill Company, 1937.

Jeffries, Ona Griffin. *In and Out of the White House . . . from Washington to the Eisenhowers.* New York: Wilfred Funk, Inc., 1960.

Jensen, Amy LaFollette. *The White House and Its Thirty-Four Families.* New York, Toronto, London: McGraw-Hill Book Company, 1965.

Johnson, Frances Ann. *Franklin Pierce 14th President.* The State of New Hampshire Recreation Division, 1953.

Johnson, Lady Bird. *A White House Diary.* New York: Holt, Rinehart and Winston, 1970.

Kane, Joseph N. *Facts About the Presidents.* 2nd ed. New York: The H. W. Wilson Co., 1968.

Kellogg, George T., editor. *The Inaugurations of all the United States Presidents George Washington to Lyndon B. Johnson.* Washington: Colortone Press.

Kimmel, Stanley. *Mr. Lincoln's Washington.* New York: Bramhall House, 1957.

Kittler, Glenn D. *Hail to the Chief! The Inauguration Days of Our Presidents.* Philadelphia and New York: Chilton Books, 1965.

Klapthor, Margaret Brown et al. *The First Ladies Cook Book.* New York: Parents' Magazine Press, 1966 edition.

Lengyel, Cornel. *Presidents of the U.S.A.: Profiles and Pictures.* New York: Bantam Books, Inc., 1961.

Lincoln, Evelyn. *My Twelve Years with John F. Kennedy.* New York: D. McKay Co., 1965.

Logan, Mrs. John A. (Mary S.), editor. *Thirty Years in Washington or Life and Scenes in Our National Capital.* Hartford, Conn.: A. D. Worthington & Co., Publishers, 1901.

Longworth, Alice Roosevelt. *Crowded Hours.* New York, London: Charles Scribner's Sons, 1933.

Lorant, Stefan. *Lincoln: A Picture Story of His Life.* New York: W. W. Norton & Company, Inc., 1969.

Manchester, William. *The Death of a President.* New York: Harper & Row, Publishers, 1967.

Nesbitt, Henrietta. *White House Diary.* Garden City, N.Y.: Doubleday & Co., Inc., 1948.

Nicolay, John G. and John Hay. "Abraham Lincoln: A History. Lincoln's Inauguration." *Century Magazine.* Vol. XXXV, 1887.

Orton, Vrest. *Calvin Coolidge's Unique Vermont Inauguration.* Plymouth, Vermont: The Calvin Coolidge Memorial Foundation, Inc., 1970.

Parks, Lillian Rogers. *My Thirty Years Backstairs at the White House.* In collaboration with Frances Spatz Leighton. New York: Fleet Publishing Corporation, 1961.

Pearce, Mrs. John N. *The White House*. As revised and enlarged by William V. Elder III and James R. Ketchum. Washington, D.C.: White House Historical Association with the cooperation of the National Geographic Society, 1966.

Poore, Ben: Perley. *Perley's Reminiscences of Sixty Years in the National Metropolis*. Philadelphia: Hubbard Brothers, Publishers, 1886. 2 vols.

Presidential Inaugurations. A Selected List of References. Compiled by Ruth S. Freitag. Washington: The Library of Congress, 1969.

Quincy, Eliza S. (Morton). *Memoir of the life of Eliza S. M. Quincy*. Boston (printed by J. Wilson), 1861.

Rayback, Robert J. *Millard Fillmore: Biography of a President*. Buffalo: Buffalo Historical Society Publications, v. 40, 1959.

Roosevelt, Franklin D. *F.D.R. His Personal Letters 1928-1945*. Edited by Elliott Roosevelt. New York: Duell, Sloan & Pearce, 1950.

Roosevelt, James, and Sidney Shalett. *Affectionately, F.D.R.* New York: Harcourt, Brace and Company, 1959.

Rosenberger, Homer T. "Inauguration of President Buchanan a Century Ago." *Records of the Columbia Historical Society*. Washington, D.C.: The Columbia Historical Society, 1961.

Salinger, Pierre. *With Kennedy*. New York: Doubleday & Company, Inc., 1966.

Sandburg, Carl. *Abraham Lincoln. The Prairie Years and The War Years*. New York: Harcourt, Brace & World, Inc., 1954.

Schlesinger, Arthur M., Jr. *A Thousand Days; John F. Kennedy in the White House*. Boston: Houghton Mifflin Co., 1965.

Seaton, Josephine. *William Winston Seaton*. Boston: J. R. Osgood & Co., 1871.

Shaw, Maud. *White House Nannie*. New York: The New American Library, Inc., 1966.

Singleton, Esther. *The Story of the White House*. 2 vols. New York: The McClure Company, 1907.

Slayden, Ellen Maury. *Washington Wife. Journal of Ellen Maury Slayden from 1897-1919*. New York and Evanston: Harper & Row, Publishers, 1963.

Smith, Margaret Bayard. *The First Forty Years of Washington Society*. Edited by Gaillard Hunt. New York: Frederick Ungar Publishing Co., reprinted from the first edition, published by Charles Scribner's Sons, 1906.

Smith, Page. *John Adams* (Vol. II). Garden City, New York: Doubleday & Company, Inc., 1962.

Sorensen, Theodore C. *Kennedy*. New York: Harper & Row, 1965.

Stryker, Lloyd P. *Andrew Johnson: a study in courage*. New York: Macmillan Co., 1929.

Taft, Mrs. William Howard (Helen Herron). *Recollections of Full Years*. New York: Dodd, Mead & Company, 1914.

Thayer, Mary Van Rensselaer. *Jacqueline Bouvier Kennedy*. Garden City, New York: Doubleday & Company, Inc., 1961.

Trollope, Mrs. Frances. *Domestic Manners of the Americans*. Edited by Donald

Smalley. New York: Vintage Books, A Division of Random House (By arrangement with Alfred A. Knopf, Inc., 1949).

Truman, Harry S. *Memoirs.* 2 vols. Garden City, New York: Doubleday & Company, 1955-56.

Truman, Margaret. *Souvenir.* New York, Toronto, London: McGraw-Hill Book Company, Inc., 1956.

Watson, Elkanah. *Men and Times of the Revolution; or, Memoirs of Elkanah Watson.* Edited by his son, Winslow C. Watson. New York: Dana and Company, Publishers, 1856.

Wharton, Anne Hollingsworth. *Social Life in the Early Republic.* Philadelphia and London: J. P. Lippincott Company, 1902.

Wharton, Anne Hollingsworth. *Through Colonial Doorways.* Philadelphia: J. B. Lippincott Company, 1893.

White, Theodore. *The Making of the President 1964.* New York: Atheneum Publishers, 1965.

Whitman, Walt. *Specimen Days In America.* London: George Routledge & Sons, Limited, New York: E. P. Dutton & Co., 1912.

Whitton, Mary Ormsbee. *First First Ladies 1789-1865.* New York: Hastings House, 1948.

Wilcox, Ansley. *How Theodore Roosevelt became President of the United States in Buffalo, September 14, 1901.* Manuscript. Buffalo: Roosevelt Memorial Association, 1919 (Reprint).

Wilcox, Pauline Burke. *Emily Donelson of Tennessee.* 2 vols. Richmond, Virginia: Garret and Massie, Inc.

Willets, Gilson. *Inside History of the White House.* New York: The Christian Herald, 1908.

Wilson, Rufus Rockwell. *Washington the Capital City.* 2 vols. Philadelphia & London: J. B. Lippincott Company, 1902.

Wolff, Perry S. *A Tour of the White House with Mrs. John F. Kennedy.* Garden City, New York: Doubleday & Company, Inc., 1962.

Manuscript papers of Augustus John Foster, Library of Congress.

Manuscript papers of Thomas Jefferson, Library of Congress.

Manuscript papers of Andrew Johnson, Library of Congress.

Manuscript papers (on microfilm) of James K. Polk, Library of Congress.

Manuscript papers of Anna Maria Brodeau Thornton (Mrs. William), Library of Congress.

Motion picture newsreels of inaugurations, National Archives.

Files or excerpts of the following:

PERIODICALS

Century Magazine

Congressional Record

Frank Leslie's Illustrated Newspaper

Frank Leslie's Popular Monthly

Gleason's Pictorial Drawing Room Companion
Harper's Bazar
Harper's New Monthly Magazine
Harper's Weekly
Ladies' Magazine and Literary Gazette
LIFE
Look
Newsweek
Senate Journal
TIME
Virginia Magazine of History

NEWSPAPERS

Boston Globe
Buffalo Courier
Buffalo Express
Cincinnati Commercial
Columbia Register (New-Haven)
Commercial Advertiser
The Connecticut Courant
The Daily Graphic (New York)
The Daily Herald (New-Haven)
The Daily National Intelligencer (Washington)
Evening Mail Illustrated
The Evening Star (Washington)
The Globe (Washington)
Illustrated London News
The Independent
Louisville Courier-Journal
Louisville Journal
Maryland Gazette (Annapolis)
The Monitor (Washington)
Nashville Republican
The National Intelligencer (Washington)
The New York Herald
New York Illustrated News
New York Sun
The New York Times
The Ohio News (Hillsborough)
The Philadelphia National Gazette
Reading Gazette
The United States Telegraph
The Virginia Gazette
Washington Daily News
The Washington Post
The Washington Star
The Washington Times-Herald

INDEX

☆ ☆ ☆